The Cambridge Manuals of Science and
Literature

EARLY RELIGIOUS POETRY OF

THE HEBREWS

T0364304

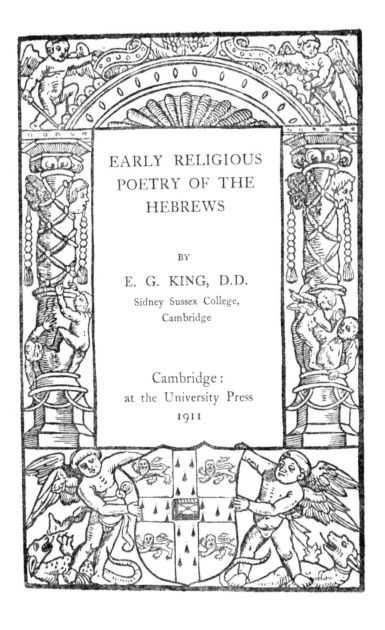

EARLY RELIGIOUS POETRY OF THE HEBREWS

BY

E. G. KING, D.D.

Sidney Sussex College,
Cambridge

Cambridge:
at the University Press
1911

CAMBRIDGE UNIVERSITY PRESS
Cambridge, New York, Melbourne, Madrid, Cape Town,
Singapore, São Paulo, Delhi, Tokyo, Mexico City

Cambridge University Press
The Edinburgh Building, Cambridge CB2 8RU, UK

Published in the United States of America by Cambridge University Press, New York

www.cambridge.org
Information on this title: www.cambridge.org/9781107605947

© Cambridge University Press 1911

First Edition 1911
First paperback edition 2011

A catalogue record for this publication is available from the British Library

ISBN 978-1-107-60594-7 Paperback

*With the exception of the coat of arms
at the foot, the design on the title page is a
reproduction of one used by the earliest known
Cambridge printer, John Siberch, 1521*

INTRODUCTION

THE title "*Early Religious Poetry of the Hebrews*" needs a further definition. It is intended to embrace the Poetry of Old Testament times as distinguished from the Poetry of the Synagogue. This will fix our period. But what are we to understand by *Religious Poetry*?

The Poet is the man whose whole being is in touch with those voices of God that we call "Nature." He may, or he may not, be a religious man. In other words, he may, or he may not, recognise the Source of those voices. The Prophet, on the other hand, is the man whose whole being is in touch with the voices of God in Humanity. He must be, more or less, a poet, in the sense in which we have defined the word, but his chief sphere will be the poetry of life. His message will necessarily be conditioned by the age in which he lives. He has his treasure in an "earthen vessel" and "he prophesies in part."

This that is true of individuals is also true of nations. Each nation has its peculiar gift, and Israel is the Prophet of Humanity. When, therefore, we speak of the *Religious Poetry* of Israel we include the whole outcome of that probation whereby the Suffering Nation was fitted to prepare the world for God. Thus, for example, there is little that is *"religious"* in the Song of Deborah or even in David's lamentation for Saul and Jonathan, but, from our point of view, all such poems must be included, marking, as they do, a stage in Israel's life.

We now turn to the outward form whereby Hebrew poetry is distinguished. I have no desire to repeat at length what has been so often written on *parallelism* as a feature of Hebrew poetry. And yet a word must be said. Parallelism may take the unsatisfying form of identity when it becomes a mere echo; though this too may be effective, e.g. Is. xv. 1 :

> In a níght 'tis destróyed, Ar-Móab is rúined.
> In a níght 'tis destróyed, Kir-Móab is rúined.

More frequently the words are varied while the thought remains the same, e.g. Prov. iii. 9 :

> Honour the Lord with thy wealth,
> And with chiefest of all thine increase.

At other times the parallelism adds to the thought either by way of development or antithesis.

Or again, the parallelism may be alternate when it suggests the strophe, e.g. Ps. lxx. 5 :

> (a)   As for mé—the póor-one, the needy !—
> (b)   Speed tó me, O Gód.
> (a₁) My Hélper, Delivérer, Thóu !
> (b₁)   O Jáhve deláy not.

The "riddle" of Samson (Judg. xiv. 14, 18):

(a)   Oút of the féeder came fóod
(b)   And oút of the fiérce there came swéetness

is answered by completing the parallelism thus :

(b₁)   Whát is there swéeter than hóney ?
(a₁)   And whát can be fiércer than líon ?

It is just this symmetry of thought that satisfies not the ear alone but also the mind, and gives such dignity and grace to Hebrew poetry. Kautzsch (*Die Poesie und die poetischen Bücher des A. T.* p. 6 f.) well points out the analogy between rhyme and parallelism by quoting from *Faust*, Part II, the words of Helena which, in Latham's translation, run thus :

"Manifold marvels do I see and hear.
Amazement smites me, much I fain would ask.
Yet would I be enlightened why the speech
Of this man rang so strange, so strange yet pleasing.
It seemed as did one tone unto another
Fit itself, fell one word upon the ear,
And straight another came to dally with it."

[See the whole passage.]

If, in the last line but one, we substitute *sentence* for *word* we have, as Kautzsch says, the secret of parallelism.

"That which the Prince of Poets here reveals as to the nature of *Rhyme*, that it is the outcome of a certain inner compulsion, applies also to the *Parallelism of Members* in Hebrew Poetry. Thus, of it too we may say :

> Scarce has a *sentence* fallen on the ear
> When straight another comes to fondle it."

He also quotes Herder as saying : "Does not all rhythm, dance and harmony, yes every charm both of shape and sound, depend upon symmetry? The two members strengthen, raise, confirm one another in their teaching or joy. In didactic poetry one saying confirms the other. It is as though the father spoke to his sons and the mother repeated it."

With this rhyme of thought the Hebrew poet did not need the rhyme of words, though the Hebrew language with its pronominal affixes would have easily lent itself to rhyme. Indeed, at times it comes unsought (e.g. Ps. vi., liv. 3 f.; Job x. 9—18, &c.). It could not be otherwise. But it is an entire mistake to suppose that rhyme was ever consciously sought by any Hebrew poet of Old Testament times.

The same may be said of *metre* if, by that term, we denote the measured beat of long and short syllables. The metre that is most common in Hebrew poetry is that of three accented syllables in parallelism. This we indicate by $(3 + 3)$. Some writers on Hebrew poetry have called these verses *hexameters*, but such a term leads us to count syllables instead of accents. I shall therefore avoid it. No doubt there are instances in which the (3 + 3) metre might, with a little careful reading, be scanned as hexameter, but this is not due to the measure of the syllables but to the stress of the accent.

Thus, if we take the line Prov. xxiv. 30 and read it strictly by the accents, passing as lightly as possible over all other syllables, it would run as follows :

> al-ṣ'déh ish-'atzél 'avárti | v'al-kérem adám ḥ'sar-lév.

I should translate this :

> I pássed by the fiéld of a slúggard | by a víne that belónged to a fóol.

The passage continues as follows :

> And ló ! 'twas grown óver with rúbbish | and the fénce of its stónes was thrown dówn.

The difficult word for "*rubbish*" gave rise to a gloss "*nettles had covered its face.*"

From this point the metre becomes irregular and we see that the text has been influenced by a quotation from Prov. vi. 10 :

> As for mé I láid it to heárt ; | I sáw and recéived instrúction.
> A little sleep, a little slumber,
> A little folding of hands for repose ;
> Then cómes along stríding thy póverty | and thy néed as a mán with a shiéld.

It would be easy to find verses that would scan, e.g. Ps. liv. 3 :

> Elohím b'shim'ká hoshíéyni
> Ubigvúrath'ká t'dínéyni.

Nor would it be difficult to find hexameters and pentameters, e.g. in the Balaam poems: but, for my part, I agree with Mr Cobb, who, after carefully examining the regular and irregular forms, writes as follows:

"What shall we say to these things? Surely we cannot continue to say that English verse is parallel with Hebrew. Nothing like this was ever written in English in the name of poetry unless by Walt Whitman....If all the poetry of the Hebrew Bible were stored in our memories, we could point to nothing more metrically regular than are some of the Psalms which have been before us, and to nothing less regular than are others of those Psalms. But it would be a mistake to suppose that the two classes are equal in extent; the irregular poems greatly predominate" (*Systems of Hebrew Metre*, p. 30).

It is highly probable that Hebrew "metre" consisted, not in long and short syllables but in the rhythmical beat of the accent. It is in this sense that I shall use the word metre as applied to Hebrew in the following pages. In dealing with the irregularities of Hebrew metre the question naturally arises as to the correctness of the text. But the knowledge of Hebrew verse is not yet sufficiently advanced to justify us in correcting the text in favour of any metrical theory unless we can support the change on independent grounds. In the chapters which follow we shall have occasion, from time to time, to offer a few suggestions on this subject.

The following facts greatly increase the difficulty of determining the laws of Hebrew verse.

(1) We cannot be sure that the Masoretic vowels and accents represent the ancient pronunciation of the language.

Strictly speaking, each word has one accent which is either *ultimate* or *penultimate*; but, in poetry, some of the longer words may have a subsidiary accent which falls on an earlier syllable, e.g. *lĕgár-gĕrothéka*, Prov. i. 9.

Where two words are joined together by a hyphen called *Maqqef* the former loses its accent: but the Masoretic use of *Maqqef* cannot be trusted in Hebrew poetry; it is often omitted when it ought to be used and used when it ought to be omitted.

(2) The duplicate texts that have come down to us (e.g. Ps. xiv. with Ps. liii.; Ps. xl. 13—17 with Ps. lxx.; Ps. lx. 5—12 with Ps. cviii.; Ps. lxxi. 1—3 with Ps. xxxi. 1 ff.; Ps. cviii. 1—5 with Ps. lvii. 7—11; 2 Sam. xxii. with Ps. xviii.) shew that the Divine Names constantly changed and that, in many other respects, the text was not accurately preserved.

Those who are familiar with the changes that have taken place in popular Hymns will easily understand that the Hebrew Psalter would be specially liable to change.

Though rhyme is only an accident in Hebrew poetry, *assonance* and *paronomasia* play an important part, and since it is impossible to reproduce the effect in a translation, it will be necessary here to give some examples in the original. The pitiful cry of the final *î* (pronounced like a long *e* as in *me*) is frequent in lamentation. Thus the lament of David over Absalom is far more pathetic in the original, which we may transliterate as follows :

> B'nî Abshālóm, b'nî b'nî Abshālóm !
> Mî yittên mūthî, ănî tachtēka,
> Abshalóm b'nî b'nî !

The same effect is very frequent in the Book of Job. We have also an instance in the Song of Lamech (Gen. iv. 23), clearly shewing that the Song, at all events in its original form, was no triumph-song but an elegy. Thus :

> Ādā v'Tzillā shemā'an qolî
> Nĕshê-Lemek ha'ăzēna imrathî
> Kî ısch haragti lĕphitẓî
> V'yéled l'chabūrathî.

We may also (with Kautzsch) note the mocking sound *ēnu* in Judg. xvi. 24, where the Philistines, rejoicing over the fall of Samson, say "Our God hath given into our hand our enemy, that laid waste our land, and that multiplied our slain." In the original thus :

> Nathan elohēnu beyadēnu eth-oyĕvēnu
> V'eth machariv artzēnu
> Va'asher hirbā eth-ch'lalēnu.

We can scarcely suppose that these words were actually used by the Philistines. The recurring *ēnu* suggests the peevish cry of children ; and, indeed, the words must have been intended to mock the speakers.

The language of Jeremiah expresses at times the very depths of sorrow. Thus Jer. viii. 18 :

> Mablígithí 'ăláy yăgón | 'ālái libí davái.

Read slowly and note the *spondee* effect of the last three words.

We may translate thus :

> Would I cómfort mysélf against sórrow | my heárt—in mé—is fáint.

The heart and courage that should support him is itself a source of weakness ; for, as he goes on to say :

> Hárvest is pást—Súmmer is énded—And wé are unsáved !

Assonance and *paronomasia* often render translation quite inadequate, e.g. Gen. ix. 27 :

> *Yaft* Elohím l' *Yéfeth* | v'yishkón b'a'hălí-Shem.
> "God shall enlarge Japheth and he shall dwell in the tents of Shem " (E.V.).

Here we have not merely the play upon the name *Japheth* but also, I think, a double meaning given to the name *Shem*, which may signify "renown" (Num. xvi. 2).

Sometimes in addition to *assonance* we have the root-meaning of a verb brought out, as when Isaiah (vii. 9) says :

Im lo tha'amīnu ki lo thēamēnu.
"If ye will not believe, surely ye shall not be established" (E.V.).

Here the verb *aman* "to believe" is used in two *voices* with a deep inner meaning which we might paraphrase

"If ye will not *stay yourselves* (on God), ye shall not be *stayed up.*"

In my translations I have done my best to imitate the rhythm of the Hebrew, but I must ask the reader kindly to bear in mind the fact that the terseness of Hebrew renders translation difficult, especially in the short lines of verse. In a little book, like the present, notes on the translation would, for the most part, be out of place ; I fear, therefore, that I may, at times, appear to be unduly dogmatic. This must be pardoned from the necessity of the case.

I have translated the Tetragrammaton by *Jáhve* simply because *Jehovah* is an impossible form and *Jáhve* has passed into common use. I have also assumed the popular pronunciation with *penultimate*

accent, although, if such a name existed, its accent
ought to be *ultimate*. In the same way I have
adopted the English pronunciation of many proper
names, e.g. *Déborah* instead of the Hebrew *Děbōráh*.
Since Hebrew poetry does not depend upon long
and short syllables but upon the beat of the accent,
I must ask the reader strictly to observe the accents
which I have marked in my translations.

E. G. K.

18 *January*, 1911.

CONTENTS

CHAPTER I

THE EARLIEST POETRY

THE English reader who knows how the language of Chaucer differs from that of Shakespeare will naturally expect the earliest poetry of the Hebrews to be clearly marked by archaisms. It is well therefore to state at once that this is not the case. Of course there are archaic forms, but fragments of Songs and popular poetry which have been preserved in the Hexateuch have come down to us in the language of the Prophetic Writers of the 8th century B.C. Thus, the Song of Lamech (Gen. iv. 23 f.), reads as follows :

> "Áda and Tzíllah, | Héar my voíce ;
> Wíves of Lámech | heárken to my spéech :
> For a mán I have sláin to my woúnd ;
> A yoúth to my húrt.
> If sévenfold véngeance be Cáin's
> Then Lámech's be séventy-séven."

If these words had been the actual words of Lamech they would have been not merely archaic but probably not even Semitic. In point of fact they

are pure Hebrew written in the *Ḳînah* or elegiac
measure of which we shall have occasion hereafter to
speak.   It is quite probable that the Song was
founded upon some Kenite (Cain) tradition connected
with the discovery of metal weapons (cf. *v.* 22) ; for
the Kenites were the smiths of the ancient world.
But the Song in *its present form* is due to the
Jehovist, i.e. to a prophetic writer of the 8th century
B.C. whose object is to trace the downward course
of the race of Cain to this Lamech, the *seventh* from
Adam shewing the fruits of murder augmented from
"seven-fold" to "seventy times seven."

It is interesting to note that in Gen. v. 29 (which
is also assigned to a Jehovistic writer) we read of the
other Lamech, of the race of Seth, "...and he called
his name *Noah*, saying, This one shall *comfort*
(√NHM) us for our works and for the toil of our
hands from the ground which Jahve hath cursed."

The Hebrew words for *"vengeance"* (NḲM) and
"comfort" (NHM) are practically identical in sound.
The good Lamech of the line of Seth inherits
"comfort," the bad Lamech of the line of Cain inherits
"vengeance."

If we omit the two last lines Lamech's song is a
complete elegy (*Ḳînah*).   I suggest that a Prophetic
Writer (the J³ of the critics) found this poem in
some collection of Kenite folk-songs, and, caring
little for poetry, but much for edification, added the

two last prosaic lines to make out his allusion to
Gen. iv. 15.

Another instance of ancient poetry which appears
to have degenerated into prose is the quotation from
the Book of Jashar in Josh. x. 12 f.:

> "Sun stand thou still upon Gibeon;
> And thou moon in the valley of Ajalon."

It is difficult to believe that a poet would have
written, *Shémesh b'Gibyón dóm*, with two accented
syllables in painful juxtaposition, when, by changing
the order of the words, he might have written the
musical line, *Shémesh dóm b'Gibyón*.   As to the
words which follow, "*So the sun stood still and the
moon stayed*," &c., they appear to be simply prose.

The amount of secular poetry in Israel must, at
one time, have been very great: thus of Solomon
alone it is said, "And he spake three thousand
proverbs, and his songs were a thousand and five.
And he spake of trees, from the cedar tree that is
in Lebanon even unto the hyssop that springeth out
of the wall,..." [1 Kings v. 12 f. (iv. 32 f.)]

Poetry is older than prose; and, in ancient Israel,
every impassioned thought expressed itself in song.
"It was indispensable to the sports of peace, it was
a necessity for the rest from the battle, it cheered
the feast and the marriage (Is. v. 12 ; Amos vi. 5 ;
Judg. xiv.), it lamented in the hopeless dirge for the
dead (2 Sam. iii. 33), it united the masses, it blessed

the individual, and was everywhere the lever of
culture. Young men and maidens vied with one
another in learning beautiful songs, and cheered with
them the festival gatherings of the villages, and the
still higher assemblies at the sanctuary of the tribes.
The maidens at Shilo went yearly with songs and
dances into the vineyards (Judg. xxi. 19), and those
of Gilead repeated the sad story of Jephtha's daughter
(Judg. xi. 40); the boys learned David's lament over
Jonathan (2 Sam. i. 18); shepherds and hunters at
their evening rests by the springs of the wilderness
sang songs to the accompaniment of the flute (Judg. v.
11). The discovery of a fountain was the occasion of
joy and song (Num. xxi. 17). The smith boasted
defiantly of the products of his labour (Gen. iv. 23).
Riddles and witty sayings enlivened the social meal
(Judg. xiv. 12; 1 Kings x.). Even into the lowest
spheres the spirit of poetry wandered and ministered
to the most ignoble pursuits (Is. xxiii. 15 ff.)[1]."

But, however much we may regret the fact, the
secular poetry of Israel has not survived, except only
in those cases where it was taken over into the service
of Religion.

At a very early date the poetry of Israel, which
had lived from mouth to mouth, was collected in
a written form. One of these collections was called

---

[1] Reuss, Art. "Heb. Poesie," Herzog. *Encykl.* quoted by Briggs.

The Book of the wars of Jahve, which is quoted in Num. xxi. 14—a very obscure passage. Two other Songs are given in the same context (Num. xxi. 17 f. and xxi. 27 ff.), one being the *Song of the Well* and the other a taunt-song recounting a defeat of the Moabites. This latter song is introduced by the words *"They that make taunt-songs say...."*

Kautzsch suggests that both these songs, and possibly the groundwork of the Songs of Moses and of Miriam (Ex. xv.), may have been preserved in this *Book of the wars of Jahve*. Some also have supposed that the words of Moses (Num. xi. 35 f.) on the journeying and resting of the Ark were found in the same source.

Another collection of similar date was *The Book Jashar*, literally *The Book of the Upright*, i.e. *of Israel* (?). This Book is quoted twice. First, as the origin of Joshua's prayer (Josh. x. 12):

> "Sún; stand thou stíll upon Gíbeon,
> And thou Móon in the válley of Ájalon";

and secondly, for David's lament over Saul and Jonathan, which must be considered later at length.

These are the only passages in which the *Book of Jashar* is mentioned in our present Hebrew text, but some have supposed, from the Septuagint text (1 Kings viii. 12 f., Greek 3 Kings viii. 53 f.), that the words of Solomon at the Dedication of the Temple were also preserved in the Book of Jashar. These words might be rendered:

> Jahve thoúght to dwéll in thick-dárkness!
> I have buílt Thee a Hoúse of Exaltátion,
> A Hóme for Thy éndless Dwélling.

Solomon feels that the Temple is to mark a new stage in the ever-growing nearness of God. He, Who, in earlier times, dwelt in the *"thick-darkness"* (Ex. xx. 21; Deut. iv. 11, v. 22), would now dwell in the midst of His people.

The word I have translated *"Exaltation"* signifies *"high-dwelling."* Similar names are given to many Babylonian temples, e.g. *E-Sagila*, "the lofty House," *E-Anna* "the House of Heaven," *E-Zida*, "the fixed House," &c.

THE SONG OF DEBORAH.

The history, date and text.

It was probably about the year 1200 B.C. when the Northern Tribes were reduced to servitude by a powerful king named Sisera, possibly a Hittite, who headed a federation of "the Kings of Canaan." The plain of Esdraelon gave great advantage to his numerous horsemen and "chariots of iron"; so "for twenty years he mightily oppressed the children of Israel" (Judg. iv. 3). The deliverance came through

Deborah, Israel's Joan of Arc, a woman of the Tribe of Issachar (Judg. v. 15), who first stirred up her fellow-tribesman, Barak, and through him the Tribes of Issachar, Ephraim, Benjamin, West Manasseh, Zebulun and Naphtali. Judah is not mentioned, and seems at this time to have been of little importance ; Reuben, Gad, Dan and Asher refused the call. The six loyal Tribes met Sisera in the plain. The first of the many battles of Esdraelon, in the valley of Megiddo, resulted in a decisive victory which established not merely the security of Israel in the North but which also tended greatly to its religious unity.

The Song of Deborah which commemorates this victory, whether actually composed by her or not, is recognised by almost every critic as belonging to the age of the events which it records. It is undoubtedly far older than the prose version which is contained in Judg. iv. from which, indeed, it differs in some important points which need not now be discussed. The Song contains archaic forms, one of the most important being the verb in *v.* 7, which has given rise to the mistaken translation "Until that *I*, Deborah, *arose.*" The text is, in parts, corrupt ; indeed Kautzsch goes so far as to say that *vv.* 8—14 "are nothing but a heap of puzzling ruins[1]."

[1] In a work like the present critical notes would be out of place. The Biblical students may be referred to the following books. Moore,

Analysis of the Song.

Though we cannot strictly divide the Song into strophe and antistrophe, yet there is a relation between the Parts which should be carefully studied.

Part I (*vv.* 2, 3). *Prelude,* addressed to "kings" and "princes" of a united Israel, bidding them to "Bless Jahve" for the "devotedness" of the loyal Tribes.

Part II (*vv.* 4, 5). A meditation on the victories of Jahve at the Exodus.

Part III (*vv.* 6—8). The low estate to which Israel had sunk in the times of the writer—A contrast!

Part IV (*vv.* 9, 10). A second *Prelude,* addressed to the Rulers and Judges, bidding them to "Bless Jahve" for the "noble-devotion" of the People—Compare Part I.

Part V (*v.* 11). The "victory of Jahve" which has just been won has freed Israel like a second Exodus—Compare Part II.

Part VI (*vv.* 12—15ᵃ and 18). The high estate to which Israel has now attained—Contrast Part III.

If the Song had ended with Part VI it would have

on Judges, *Critical Edition of the Hebrew Text*; G. A. Cooke, *The History and Song of Deborah*; Kautzsch, *Literature of the Old Testament*; Zapletal, *Das Deboralied* and various articles in Hastings' *Dictionary of the Bible.*

had a certain completeness in itself. But the thought of the faithful Tribes who are praised in Part VI suggests, by way of contrast,

Part VII (vv. 15ᶜ—17). The taunt-song on the unfaithful Tribes.

Part VIII (vv. 19—22). A magnificent description of the Battle. The star-gods of Canaan fight in their orbits for Jahve. The Kishon river of Sisera's home rises in torrent to sweep him away ; and the scene ends (v. 22) in a marvellous piece of word-painting in which the Hebrew pictures the once terrible horses hammering their hoofs in headlong flight—"*da'ărôth da'ărôth abbîrâv.*" Zapletal well translates this verse

> "Da stampfen die Hüfe der Rosse ;
> Der Galopp, der Galopp der Renner !"

Part IX (vv. 23—27) records the events in the pursuit. The curse on Meroz for refusing aid and a blessing on the Kenite friend of Israel.

Part X (vv. 28—30). A taunt-song picturing the scene in Sisera's home. This, from its own point of view, is a masterpiece of irony. The text has suffered from a double reading in v. 30.

Metre.

The Ode is dithyrambic, and the metre irregular. For the most part it is 3 + 3 metre but at times it breaks into the more lively metre (2 + 2) + (2 + 2). In

the two Preludes the metre again varies. I have
endeavoured to represent this in my translation.

Part I. *Prelude.*

2   For Ísrael's whóle self-abándonment—
    For the Péople's devótedness
        Bléss ye Jáhve!

3   Héar ye kings; | heárken ye prínces;
    Í of Jáhve | Í would síng,
    Would hýmn of Jáhve | Ísrael's Gód.

Part II. *The Victories of Jahve at the Exodus.*

4   Jáhve when Thou wéntest forth from Séir,
    When Thou márchedst from the fiéld of Édom,
    The éarth did sháke | the héavens drópped,
    The véry cloúds | drópped wáter.

5   Moúntains mélted | at the présence of Jáhve,
    At the présence of Jáhve | Ísrael's Gód.

Part III. *The low estate to which Israel is reduced!*

6   In the dáys of Shamgár ben-A̯'náth
    In (*Ísrael ?*) róads were desérted.
    They stóle along by býways, | twísting lánes.

7   Víllage-life (?) ceased, | In Ísrael they céased,
    Till Déborah róse | as a Móther in Ísrael.

8   (*The first two lines are corrupt and the whole verse seems*
      out of place.)

    .   .   .   .

    Was there shiéld or dárt to be séen
    'Mid the fórty thoúsand of Ísrael?

PART IV. *A second Prelude.*

9   My heárt is to Ísrael's léaders
    The Péople's nóbly-devóted-ones,
        Bléss ye Jáhve!
10 Ye that ríde on white ásses—
    Ye that sít on the dívan
    Or that wálk by the wáy
    ......(*Muse upon your deliverance*(?)).

PART V. *The victorious work of Jahve in the present.*

11 From the twáng of the árchers | at the pláces for wáter,
    Thére let them célebrate | the víctories of Jáhve,
    His víctories for víllage-life (?) in Ísrael.
    Nów there can gó to the gátes | a Péople of Gód.

PART VI. *In contrast with Part III.*

12 Awáke, awáke, Debórah;
    Awáke, awáke, utter sóng;
    Ríse up Bárak, | lead captive thy cáptors | thou són of
        Abinóam.

        .   .   .   .

The two verses which follow are hopelessly corrupt.
They seem to contain obscure allusions to the Tribes
of Ephraim, Machir (i.e. Manasseh), Issachar and
Zebulun who were loyal to Deborah. We pass therefore to the taunt-song directed against the stay-at-
home Tribes.

It opens with a play upon the word "*divisions*"
which might be translated "*rivers*" (as in Job xx. 17).
The *dividing rivers* of Reuben were a fit emblem of

the *divided hearts* of this "unstable" tribe (cf. Gen. xlix. 4). The word translated "*sheepfolds*" (E.V.) is only found here and in Gen. xlix. 14 where one of the Tribes is pictured as an ass crouching down between *the panniers* (not *sheepfolds* as E.V.) contented to be a burden-bearer, caring only for rest. I believe that the word carries the same taunt in the Song of Deborah.

PART VII. *The taunt-song.*

15^c Amóng the divísions of Reúben
 Gréat were the séarchings of heárt.
16 Whý didst thou sít 'twixt the pánniers
 Hárking to the pípings for the flócks?
 Amóng the divísions of Reúben
 Gréat were the séarchings of heárt.
17 Gílead abode sáfe beyond Jórdan;
 And Dán—why stáyed he by shíps?
 Ashér sat stíll by his cóast-line,
 And abóde by his créeks.

A verse which would seem more in place in Part VI.

18 Zebúlun was a péople that héld life chéap,
 And Náphtali was in the fóremost fiéld.

PART VIII. *The Battle.*

19 Thén came kíngs and foúght;
 There foúght the kíngs of Cánaan.
 In Táänach by the wáters of Megíddo
 They tóok no gaín of móney.

20　From héaven foúght the stárs—
　　Foúght in their coúrses 'gainst Sísera.
21　The ríver Kíshon o'erwhélmed them,
　　The tórrent-ríver of Kíshon.
　　[My soúl march ón with stréngth !]
22　Thén were the hórse-hoofs hámmered
　　By his gálloping gálloping rácers[1].

PART IX. *Events in the pursuit.*

23　Cúrse ye Méroz, saith Jáhve ;
　　Cúrse ye her dwéllers with cúrsing ;
　　That they cáme not to Jáhve's hélp,
　　To Jáhve's hélp 'gainst the míghty.
24　Bléssed by wómen be Jáel
　　The wífe of Héber the Kénite ;
　　By wómen in the tént is she bléssed.
25　Wáter he ásked, | mílk she gáve ;
　　She óffered bútter | in a lórdly dísh.
26　She laíd her hánd to the tént-pin,
　　Her ríght to the wórkman's hámmer.
　　She strúck him woúnding his héad,
　　Piércing and stríking through his témples.
27　He sánk, he féll, he láy ;
　　At her féet he sánk, he féll ;
　　Whére he sánk he shattéred féll !

PART X. *The scene shifts to Sisera's home.*

28　The móther of Sísera | oút through the láttice
　　Péers through the wíndow | and gléefully cálls,
　　"Whý does his cháriot | cóme so slów ?
　　Why tárries the tréad of his téam ?"

[1] Jer. viii. 16, xlvii. 3.

29   Her ládies, her wísest, replý,
       Yea shé hersélf | ánswers hersélf;
30   "Áre they not fínding, | divíding the spoíl,
       Doúble embroídery | for the héad of the héro,
       A spoíl of dyed gárments for Sísera,
       A spoíl of dyed gárments and 'broídery,
       Of doúble embroídery for the néck of...."

The contrast between the Sisera lying dead with stricken temples and the Sisera that his mother expected, triumphant "*in dyed garments*," is grim indeed.

An early copyist evidently wrote rḥm rḥmthym, i.e. "*a womb two wombs*," instead of rkm rḳmthym, i.e. "*embroidery double embroidery*" which occurs later in the same verse. This has given rise to the unfortunate translation "a damsel or two" (E.V. and R.V.). The last two lines of *v.* 30 are little more than duplicates of the two preceding lines and may have originated in this way.

One other example of the most ancient poetry, dating from about 1120 B.C., is Jotham's *Fable of the trees* (Judg. ix. 8—15) with its splendid irony.

This Fable of Jotham is undoubtedly in verse, the metre being in three beats as follows :

         The trées went fórth on a tíme
         To anoínt for thémselves a kíng,
         And they saíd to the Ólive, Rule ó'er us.

But to thém the Ólive replíed,
"Shoúld I then léave my rich-oíl,
Whereby góds and mén get hónour,
And gó to wáve o'er the trées?"

Thén said the trées to the Fíg-tree
Come thóu and bé our quéen.
But the fíg-tree saíd unto thém,
"Shoúld I then leáve my swéetness
And that próduce of míne so góodly
And gó to wáve o'er the trées?"

Thén said the trées to the Víne,
Come thoú and bé our quéen.
But the víne made ánswer to thém;
"Shoúld I then léave my víntage,
That gláddens both góds and mén,
And gó to wáve o'er the trées?"

Thén said the trées to the Brámble,
Come thoú and be kíng over ús.
So the brámble replíed to the trées;
"Íf ye are trúly anoínting
Mé as a kíng over yoú
Then cóme ye, repóse in my shádow;
If nót, let come fíre from the brámble
And devoúr the cédars of Lébanon."

The reader will notice that the olive, fig, and vine
reply in the same metre $(3 + 3 + 3)$, whereas the
pompous answer of the bramble is lengthened out
into five lines $(3 + 3 + 3 + 3 + 3)$.

We now pass over a period of about one hundred
years of silence till we come to the hero-age of David

(*c.* 1000 B.C.) "the darling of Israel's Songs" (2 Sam.
xxiii. 1); David alike pre-eminent in music and in
war.   The very greatness of David's work creates a
difficulty ; for, as all Law centres round the name
of Moses, its originator, so well-nigh the whole of
Psalmody has been ascribed to David.   According to
Amos (vi. 5), David's name was associated with secular
poetry and with the invention of musical instruments.
Fortunately for us, David's lament over Saul and
Jonathan has been preserved.

CHAPTER II

THE POETRY OF THE EARLY KINGDOM

THE Poetry, of which specimens will be given in the present chapter may be said roughly to belong to the age of David and Solomon, though we shall have occasion to illustrate it from poems of a much later date.

The reader will kindly remember that we are only professing to give specimens and not to include or even to mention all the poems that might reasonably be assigned to the prolific age of David and Solomon.

David's Elegy on Saul and Jonathan.

This lovely poem was taken, by the Editor of the Books of Samuel, from the lost *Book of Jashar*. It is undoubtedly genuine. It breathes the spirit of the highlander grieving for brave comrades slain on their own mountains by the despised and hated Philistine of the lowlands.

We shall first offer a translation and then it will be necessary to give a few brief notes.

(2 Sam. i. 19 ff.)

19   Thou róebuck of Ísrael ! | piérced on thine ówn mountain-
      heíghts !
    HÓW ARE THE MÍGHTY FÁLLEN !

STROPHE I.

20   Téll it nót in Gáth ;
    Annoúnce it nót in stréets of Áskelon ;
    Lést the daúghters of the Phílistines rejoíce ;
    Lést the daúghters of the uncírcumcised tríumph !

STROPHE II.

21   Ye hílls of Gilbóa be déwless !
    Ye fiélds of oblátions be raínless !
    For thére was the shiéld of héroes pollúted ;
    The shiéld of Saúl, withoút the anoínting.

STROPHE III.

22   From the blóod of the slaín—
    From the fát of the míghty—
    The bów of Jónathan túrned not báck—
    The swórd of Saúl retúrned not émpty.

STROPHE IV.

23   Saúl and Jónathan !—
    So déar so delíghtful in lífe ;—
      And in déath undivíded !
    They were swífter than éagles, | strónger than líons.

STROPHE V.

24   Ye daúghters of Ísrael—
    Wéep over Saúl
    Who clád you in scárlet | with lúxurý,
    Who décked your appárel | with jéwelrý.

25 Hów are the míghty fállen
In the mídst of the báttle!
Áh, Jónathan! | piérced on thine ówn mountain-heíghts!

STROPHE VI.

26 Woe is mé for thée, my bróther!
Jónathan to mé so déar!
Thy lóve to mé more márvellous
Than wóman's lóve.
Hów are the míghty fállen!
the wár-weapons pérished!

The word *tz'vî* (*v.* 19) must often be translated "*pride*," "*glory*," "*beauty*," or "*delight*," but it also signifies the "*roebuck*," probably so named for its "*beauty*." It is applied to Asahel (2 Sam. ii. 18) who was "light of foot as the *roebuck*." In early warfare, as we know from Homer, this was no small praise. In our poem it is evident from *v.* 25[b] that the epithet applies to Jonathan, not to Saul. Jonathan is, indeed, "*the pride*," the "*dulce decus*" of Israel; but such a translation would hide from the English reader the picture of the roebuck "pierced on its own mountain heights."

The form, *ha tz'vî*, does not mark the *def. article*, as E.V. "*The* beauty &c.," but the *vocative*; like *ha bath Jerushalaim* "O daughter of Jerusalem" (Lam. ii. 23).

It is evident that Jonathan is chiefly in David's thoughts. It is Jonathan that is styled the "roebuck

of Israel," the beautiful stag pierced and dying in its
own mountain haunts. To this thought he returns
in *v.* 25[b]. In *v.* 22 Jonathan is placed before Saul
and, in the last strophe, *v.* 26, Jonathan stands
alone.

If we omit the refrain, which is thrice repeated
(*vv.* 19, 25, 26), the poem falls naturally into six
strophes of four lines each. The two central strophes
(III and IV) contain the central thought, *the praise
of the dead*, their valour and their virtues—"Jonathan
and Saul" (*v.* 22), "Saul and Jonathan" (*v.* 23). The
strophes on either side of this central thought correspond with one another, strophe V with strophe I
and strophe VI with strophe II. Thus strophe I
pictures the "daughters of the Philistines" in their
joy, strophe V, the "daughters of Israel" in their
sorrow.

Strophes II and VI contain, I think, the most
beautiful thoughts of the Elegy; strophe II referring
to Saul, strophe VI to Jonathan. Of *Saul* (*v.* 21) he
thinks as of the *Lord's Anointed* and feels that,
where such a one has fallen, the very hills should lose
the anointing rain of their fertility. But of Jonathan
(*v.* 26) he thinks with the deepest devotion of friend-
ship. In the former case it was a "shield cast away"
(*v.* 21), but now it seems, in his grief, as though all
"weapons of war had perished" (*v.* 26). "The
religious element (says Kautzsch, *Lit. of the O.T.*) is

quite absent from the Song. But what a monument has David here raised to the king from whom he suffered so much, to the heroic youth at his side, and not less, to himself."

Briggs (*Study of Holy Scripture*, p. 381) comments on the fact that this "the earliest Hebrew dirge" is not written in the *Ḳinah* or dirge measure of which we shall speak in a later chapter. But, in this, I think he is wrong. It is quite true that it is not composed in the finished and artistic form of the later *Ḳinah*; but in the short sob-like lines of two beats which break the longer lines it seems to me that we have the *Ḳinah* measure in its earliest form. See especially *vv.* 23^c, 26^d.

The Blessing of Jacob.

We must now consider that collection of ancient poetry which goes by the name of the *Blessing of Jacob* (Gen. xlix. 2 ff.), and, for this purpose, it will suffice to select the two leading Tribes of Ephraim (Joseph) and Judah. It is impossible to give the actual date of these tribe-poems which were incorporated by the Jehovist, *c.* 850 B.C. Probably they are at least as old as the time of Solomon.

The Blessings cannot be understood without some brief reference to the position of the 12 Tribes in relation to the 12 heavenly Signs or to their position

in the "Camp" (Num. ii.). Here we read that the
Camp of Judah with its standard (the Lion?) was
to pitch "on the *east* side, toward the sunrising"
(Num. ii. 3), and the Camp of Ephraim, with its
standard (the Ox?) was to pitch on the *west* side
(Num. ii. 18). Properly Reuben, as the first-born,
ought to have occupied the higher place as is explained in 1 Chron. v. 1 f.: "Now the sons of Reuben
the firstborn of Israel (for he was the firstborn);
but forasmuch as he defiled his father's bed, the birthright was given to the sons of Joseph the son of
Israel: and the genealogy is not to be reckoned after
the birthright. For Judah prevailed over his brethren,
so that the Ruler should be from him; while the
birthright should belong to Joseph."

These words are very important as giving the
oldest comment on the *Blessing of Jacob.*

The position of Joseph on the *west* (Num. ii.)
brings him into connexion with the seventh month
(Autumnal Equinox). In Gen. xxx. 23, the Elohist
derives the name *Joseph* from the root *asaph*, "*to
gather in.*" This word *asaph* is constantly used of
the *ingathering* of the fruits of the earth, *Asaph*
being the oldest name for the *Feast of Ingathering*
(Ex. xxiii. 16, xxxiv. 22), which was held in the
seventh month. Further we note that the Elohist
(Gen. xxx. 20, 23[b]) regards Joseph as the *seventh* son,
so that if the 12 Tribes were written in the order of

the 12 Months *Joseph* would come in the 7th Month with the great *Ingathering* (*Asaph*) of the fruits of the earth.

These brief remarks are necessary in order that we may understand the Blessing which follows. Though *Joseph* is mentioned as receiving the Blessing it is evident that *Ephraim* is in the writer's mind (cf. Gen. xlviii. 20). I think it probable that the original poem began,

> A *fruitful* bough is *Ephraim*,

the name *Ephraim* being derived in Gen. xli. 52 from the Hebrew word signifying *fruitfulness*.

We now give the words of the Blessing so far as they relate to this idea of *fruitfulness*, reserving the other portion of the Blessing for later consideration.

(Gen. xlix. 22 ff.)

22   A frúitful boúgh is *Jóseph*,
       A frúitful boúgh by a spríng;
       With óffshoots o'ermóunting the wáll

       .   .   .   .
       .   .   .   .

25ᶜ   Bléssings of héaven abóve,
       Bléssings of the déep that croúcheth únder,
       Bléssings of bréasts and wómb,

       .   .   .   .
       Bléssings of the everlásting moúntains,
       The desíre of the etérnal hílls,
       May they bé upon Jóseph's héad,
       On the héad of him crówned among bróthers.

We must compare this with the Joseph-blessing in the *Song of Moses* (Deut. xxxiii.), a Poem which was probably written in the Northern Kingdom in the reign of Jeroboam II (*c.* 780 B.C.). Thus:

(Deut. xxxiii. 13 ff.)

Bléssed by Jáhve (be) his lánd
From príme of héaven's déw,
From the déep that croúcheth únder,
From the príme of the oútcome of súns,
From the príme of the oútbreak of móons,
From the chiéfest of áncient moúntains,
From the príme of etérnal hílls,
From the príme of éarth with her fúlness.

   .   .   .   .   .   .

Let them cóme upon Jóseph's héad,
On the héad of him crówned among bróthers.

The word which we have translated "*prime*" signifies the "*choicest fruit*": thus we see that the Divine thought for *Joseph* was exactly that which was expressed in the *Asaph* or *Feast of Ingathering*, viz. the summing up of all fruitfulness for the use of man and for the honour of God.

We now return to the words which we omitted when we considered the Blessing on Joseph in Gen. xlix.

23   And they bítterly véxed him and shót,
       And the árchers pursúed him with háte:
24   But his bów abóde in stréngth
       And his árms and hánds were made stróng
       By the hánds of the Míghty of Jácob.
       [From thence is the Shepherd the stone of Israel.]

In the first five lines we have a picture of "Joseph" suffering persecution but strengthened by the hand of God. This is the germ of that thought which, in later times, found expression among the Jews as Messiah ben Joseph, the suffering Messiah.

The fifth line, "From thence is the Shepherd" &c., has, I believe, never been explained. I suggest the following: The root *asaph* is used not only of the "*gathering in*" of *fruits* but also of the "*gathering in*," i.e. the "*folding*" of *sheep* (Gen. xxix. 7, 8) and is applied to God as the Shepherd *gathering in* His people like a flock (Mic. ii. 12, iv. 6).

The Second Isaiah pictures God as the Shepherd of the stars, folding them all like sheep, and draws the lesson that, much more will God be the Shepherd of Israel. Thus:

(Is. xl. 26 ff.)

> Líft up your éyes on hígh,
> And sée who creáted (all) thése;
> That márshals their hóst by númber,
> And námeth them áll by their námes;
> Through abúndance of míght
> And pówer of stréngth
> Not óne of them fáileth.

We have a similar poetical image in Browning's *Saul*:

> "...the tune all our sheep know, as one after one,
> So docile they come to the pen-door till folding be done.
> .   .   .   .
> And now one after one seeks its lodging, as star follows star
> Into eve and the blue far above us,—so blue and so far!"

There was undoubtedly a relation between the
gems which represented Israel (Ex. xxviii. 17 ff.,
xxix. 8ff.) and the "stones of fire" (Ezek. xxviii. 13f.),
i.e. the stars in the sky. As in Ezek. xxviii. the
"Cherub" that "walked up and down 'midst the stones
of fire" represented the Patron of Tyre, so in Gen.
xlix. the heavenly Patron of Israel is none other
than God Himself, who shepherds the stones of
Israel.

The thought of God as the Shepherd of Israel was
one peculiarly dear to the Prophets of the Captivity,
e.g. Jer. xxxi. 10 : "He who (now) scattereth Israel
will gather him, and will keep him as a shepherd doth
his flock" (cf. Ezek. xxxiv.).

We have traced a connexion between *Joseph* and
Asaph with the double thought of the *Ingathering*
of the fruits of the earth and the *Ingathering* by the
Good Shepherd. We have also found a hint of Joseph
as a Sufferer strengthened by God. The present
writer has shewn that a connexion exists between
the *Asaph* Psalms, the *Asaph* Feast, the House of
Joseph and the "Shepherd of Israel" (*Psalms in
Three Collections*, Part II. Introd. v. ff. Cf. Part III.
Introd. viii., x.).

One of these *Asaph* Psalms is of special interest
from a poetical point of view, not only for its beauty
of thought but also for the regularity of its rhythm
and its clear division into strophes indicated by the
thrice repeated refrain. At the risk of a slight

digression it may be well to consider it in this place.

The Hebrew text has been carefully analysed by Mr Cobb in his *Systems of Hebrew Metre*, p. 30 f. In the translation which follows, I have, for the most part, accepted his emended text.

(Ps. lxxx.)

STROPHE I.

2 Thou Shépherd of Ísrael, heárken!
  That léadest Jóseph like shéep;
  Shine fórth Thou chérub-thróned!
3 ['Fore Éphraim, Bénjamin and Manásseh[1]]
  Roúse Thy míghty stréngth
  And cóme our greát-salvátion.
4 Gód of Hósts, restóre us!
  Let shíne Thy Fáce, that we be sáved!

STROPHE II.

5 Gód of Hósts, how lóng?
  Shouldst Thou fúme 'gainst the práyer of Thy Péople?
6 Thou hast féd them with bréad of téars;
  With téars in full méasure for drínk.
7 Thou mákest us strífe to our neíghbours;
  And our énemies laúgh us to scórn.
8 Gód of Hósts, restóre us!
  Let shíne Thy Fáce, that we be sáved!

STROPHE III.

9 A víne Thou didst móve out of Égypt;
  Dríving out nátions and plánting it.

---

[1] ? Gloss.

10 Thou mádest róom; | it strúck its róots; | and fílled the
Lánd.
11 The moúntains were cláad with its sháde;
And its bránches were Gód-like cédars.
12 It pút forth its boúghs to the Séa;
And its téndrils réached to the Ríver.

STROPHE IV.

13 Whý didst Thou bréak its hédges,
So that áll that pass bý may plúck it?
14 The bóar from the wóod lays it wáste
And fíeld-creatures pásture upón it.
15 Gód of Hósts, retúrn now!
Lóok from héaven and sée.
16 Táke thoúght for this víne,
And the stém that Thy ríght-hand hath plánted,
17 It is búrned with fíre as mere fúel!

STROPHE V.

At the rebúke of Thy Fáce let them pérish.
18 Be Thy hánd on Thy ríght-hand mán;
On the Mán[1] thou madest stróng for Thysélf.
19 For we wíll not go báck from Thée:
Give us lífe, and we cáll on Thy Náme.
20 GÓD OF HÓSTS, RESTÓRE US!
LET SHÍNE THY FÁCE, THAT WE BE SÁVED!

It will be seen that the Psalm falls into five
strophes, three of which are closed by the refrain.
Very possibly the refrain originally closed all five
strophes.

[1] " Son of Man."

The best commentary on this Psalm is the *Blessing on Joseph* (Gen. xlix.).

The contents of the Psalm might be summed up briefly as follows :

Strophe I.   An Appeal to God as the Shepherd of Joseph (cf. *Blessing*, Gen. xlix. 24ᵈ).

Strophe II.   Joseph cruelly persecuted (cf. *Blessing*, Gen. xlix. 23).

Strophe III.   Joseph as the Vine of fruitfulness (cf. *Blessing*, Gen. xlix. 22, 25, 26).

Strophe IV.   Why, then, has God forsaken His Vine ?

Strophe V.   Surely Joseph implies a "Son of Man" whose arms were made strong by God ? (cf. *Blessing*, Gen. xlix. 24).

It will be seen that strophe IV answers to strophe III, strophe V to strophe II, while strophe I is a general summary of the whole Psalm.

It will, I think, be evident that we are justified in regarding the Joseph-Blessing as Messianic. The Camp of Joseph ("Ephraim, Benjamin and Manasseh," Ps. lxxx. 2, Num. ii. 18 ff.) on the *west* with its emblem of the Ox, and the Divine Name *Elohim*, with the thoughts of the *Ingathering (Asaph)*, the Asaph Psalms and the Shepherd of Israel, form a part of that conception which, at a much later time, took shape in the Jewish expectation of a "Messiah ben Joseph," who was to be a Sufferer.

We now turn to the Blessing on Judah (Gen. xlix. 9 ff.). If the order of the Tribes in the *Blessing of Jacob* be compared with the order in the four Camps (Num. ii.), it will be seen that they practically agree, except for the fact that the *Camp of Judah* (i.e. Judah, Issachar, Zebulun) has changed places with the *Camp of Reuben.* The order in the Poem is the more ancient, in other words the Camp of Judah originally belonged to the *South,* Judah coming with *Leo* at the Summer Solstice. This will explain the fact that the emblem of Judah was the *Lion.*

This point of the Cycle is also associated with the Divine Name *Yah,* the name *Judah (Yehudah)* lending itself to the Hebrew word which signifies *"praised,"* and also to the Divine Name.

The reader is asked to note the play upon the name Judah, the reference to the Lion, and, possibly, to the geographical position of the Tribe, in the Blessing which follows :

(Gen. xlix. 8 ff.)

8   *Júdah* art thoú | that thy bréthren *práise*;
     Thou láyest thine hánd | on the néck of thy fóes ;
     To thée shall bow dówn | the sóns of thy fáther.

Another fragment in different metre refers to the position of Judah in the Camps and possibly in the geography of the Land.

9   A Líon's whélp is Júdah ;
     From the préy, my són, thou art góne.
     He coúcheth repósed as a líon,
     As an óld-lion, whó shall aroúse him?

10 The scéptre depárts not from Júdah,
   Nor the stáff of swáy from befóre him,
   Untíl the cóming of Shíloh
   And the dráwing of Péoples to hím.

In this last line I follow the reading of the
Samaritan text (see also Chaldee) which suggests the
"flowing together" of the Peoples, like water. This
idea is found in Is. ii. 2 (Mic. iv. 1); Jer. li. 44; Is. lx. 5.
See also my note on Ps. xxxiv. 5 (6).

The words which follow have no apparent connexion with *v.* 10, though personally I believe the
reference to be to the mystical "Vine of Eridu,"
rather than to the suitability of Judea for the growth
of the vine. (See my notes on Pss. lxxx. 8 ff., lxxii.
16.) If this be so, *v.* 11 is also Messianic, containing,
as it does, a reference to "The Vine of David[1]."

11 Bínding his cólt to the Víne,
   The fóal of his áss to the Sórek;
   He stéeps his gárment in wíne,
   His clóthing in blóod of the grápe.

12 A dárkness of éyes through wine,
   A whíteness of téeth through mílk.

In *v.* 11 the "colt" and "the foal of the ass"
suggest Zech. ix. 9, where the Messiah is pictured
"riding upon an ass and on a colt the foal of an
ass," while the latter part of the verse suggests the
Conqueror from Edom (Is. lxiii. 1—3) with garments

[1] On the " Vine of David," see also p. 129.

stained as with the blood of the grape. Thus we have one continuous Messianic thought in *vv.* 10, 11.

We cannot compare the Judah-blessing in Gen. xlix. with the later blessing in Deut. xxxiii., as we did in the case of the Joseph-blessing, because, in the opinion of some scholars, the words (Deut. xxxiii. 7) "Hear, Jahve, the voice of *Judah,* and bring him in unto his people," should read "Hear, Jahve, the voice of *Simeon,*" with a play on the name *Simeon* which signifies "*God hath heard*" (Gen. xxix. 33).

Song of Moses (Ex. xv. 1 ff.).

The rhythm of this Song is very perfect. It consists of four beats in each line, divided in the middle by the cæsura. The first line of *v.* 14 has, it is true, only three beats ; but this, I think, is intentional and gives the effect of a *rest* in music. A good reader would pause on the word "*tremble.*"

The line which constitutes the 5th verse has, in the Hebrew, exactly the ring of a pentameter ; this I have endeavoured to reproduce in my translation.

As to strophes there is no clear indication, but the natural divisions seem to me to be after *vv.* 8, 12, 18. This gives three strophes of 12, 11, and 13 lines each. The refrain would probably be repeated at the end of each strophe (cp. Ex. xv. 21).

(Ex. xv. 1 ff.)

Refrain.

1 To JÁH IT IS I SÍNG | FOR HÉ HATH PROUDLY TRÍUMPHED:
THE HÓRSE AS WELL AS RÍDER | HE HATH THRÓWN INTO
THE SÉA.

STROPHE I, *recounting the victory of Jahve.*

2 My stréngth my song is Jáh | and Hé is my salvátion :
Súch is my God, I práise ; | my fáther's God, I extól.
3 Jáhve is a man of wár, | Jáhve is His Náme.
4 Pháraoh's chariots and hóst | He hath cást into the séa :
The choícest of his cáptains | are súnk in the Red Séa.
5 The déeps have cóvered them sínking | dówn to the dépths
like a stóne.
6 Thy ríght hand, Jáhve, | is glórious in pówer ;
Thy ríght hand, Jáhve, | breáketh the énemy.
7 In Thy éxcellent greátness | Thou destróyest Thy fóes.
Thou séndest Thy wráth | that consúmeth as stúbble.
8 With the blást of Thy nóstrils | the wáters were píled ;
Upríght as a heap stood the floóds ; | the déeps in the séa's
heart grew túrbid.

STROPHE II. *The boast of the enemy contrasted with the
triumph of Jáhve. Compare the Song of Deborah.*

9 The énemy sáid, | I pursúe, I o'ertáke ;
I pórtion the spoíl, | I sáte myself ón them ;
I dráw but my swórd, | my hánd dispossésseth them !
10 Thou didst blów with Thy wínd | the séa overcóvered them
They sánk as léad | in the míghty wáters.
11 Whó like Thée | among the góds, O Jáhve ?
Whó like Thée | glórious in hóliness ?
Célebrate in práise-songs | wórking wónders ?

K. 3

12 Thou didst strétch Thy right hánd | earth swállowed them
        úp :
13 Thou didst shépherd with Thy mércy, | this Péople Thou
        redéemest :
    Thou didst léad them on with pówer | únto Thy holy
        Dwélling.

STROPHE III. *The effect of this victory upon the Nations as
a stage in the establishment of God's kingdom upon earth.*

14 The Péoples have héard and trémble—
    Térror hath laid hóld | on Philístia's inhábitants :
15 Nów are confoúnded | (all) the dúkes of Édom :
    The míghty men of Móab | trémbling hath séized them :
    Mélted are áll | the hábitants of Cánaan :
16 Fállen upón them | is térror great and dréad.
    By the greátness of Thine árm | they are stíll as a stóne.
    To the énd that there páss | Thy Péople, O Jáhve ;
    To the énd that there páss | this Péople Thou púrchased,
17 That Thou bríngest and plántest | in the Moúnt of Thine
        héritage,
    The Pláce for Thee to dwéll | that Thóu didst make, O Jáhve,
    The Sánctuary, Lórd, | that Thine hánds estáblished.
18 Jáhve shall be Kíng | for éver and éver.

The deliverance at the Red Sea would, undoubtedly, have been celebrated in song, and the words
which we have here as the refrain may have been
the actual words used by Moses and Miriam. But
the Song, *in its present form,* belongs to a later age,
when the Sanctuary was established in Zion (see *v.* 17).
The leading thought in the Song is *the Kingship of
God upon earth, established by a Theophany.* This

will be seen more clearly if we read it in connexion with such passages as the following with which it is closely related.

An unknown Prophet (Is. xi. 15 f.) pictures the return of Israel from Assyria as a drying up of the Euphrates and a second passage of the Red Sea; and then, with the Song of Moses in his mind, he goes on to say (xii. 1 ff.) In that day thou shalt say,

> I thánk Thee, Jáhve : | tho' Thoú wast ángry with me,
> Thine íre is túrned | and Thoú dost cómfort me.
> Lo, Gód of my salvátion ! | I trúst and will not féar:
> For *My Stréngth my Song is Jáh* | *and Hé is my Salvátion.*
>
> .   .   .   .

In that day ye shall say:

> *Thánk ye Jáhve* | *Célebrate His Náme* ;
> Decláre among the Péoples His déeds ;
> Recoúnt that His Náme is exálted.
> Hýmn ye Jáhve | *for proúdly hath He dóne* :
> Let thís be néwsed | in áll the éarth.
> Crý aloud and síng | thou inhábitress of Zíon ;
> For Ísrael's Hóly-One | is greát withín thee.

In these last words the Theophany is pictured as a Divine Indwelling. This thought is developed in Ps. cxiv. which is one of the Songs of the Hallel, and belongs to the general cycle of Passover Hymns. This Psalm, of course, belongs to a later date, but it will be well to consider it now as illustrating the Song of Moses.

(Ps. cxiv.)

Strophe I.

When Ísrael cáme out of Égypt,
Jácob from bárbarous péople,
Then Júdah becáme His sánctuary,
Ísrael His séat of domínion.

Strophe II.

The Séa behéld and fléd;
Jórdan was túrned away báck;
The moúntains skípped like ráms;
The hílls like the yoúng of the flóck.

Strophe III.

What aíled thee, O Séa, that thou fléddest?
Thou Jórdan that thóu shouldst turn báck?
Ye moúntains, why skípped ye like ráms?
Ye hílls like the yoúng of the flóck?

Strophe IV.

Trávail thou Éarth at the Máster's Présence,
At the Présence of Jácob's Gód!
Who túrned the Róck into wáter-póols,
The flínt into sprínging-wáters.

In the four strophes of this Psalm the connexion
of thought is plain. Strophe I states the fact of the
Indwelling of God in His Chosen People in times
past. Strophes II and III picture the effect of this
Indwelling upon Nature; the Red Sea, the mountains,
and the Jordan recognising their God. Strophe IV

returns to the thought of strophe I. The *Divine Indwelling* is still a fact which Earth must yet recognise in the birth-pangs of a new creation. One further illustration may be taken from the Theophany in Ps. xviii. 8 ff.

8 Then éarth itself quívered and quáked,
The moúntains' foundátions were troúbled,
Yea, they quívered becaúse He was wróth.
9 There wént up a smóke from His nóstrils,
And a fíre consúmed from His moúth,
Yea flámes were kíndled therefróm.
10 So He bówed the Héavens and cáme,
With the Dárkness únder His feét.
11 He róde on the Chérub and fléw,
Came swóoping on wíngs of the wínd;
12 He máde of the dárkness His cóvert,
His pavílion all roúnd Him—
Dárkness of wáters— | dense cloúds of the skíes.
13 Through His spléndour oppósing | His dénse clouds remóved,
Háil with flámes of fíre!
14 And Jáhve thúndered in héaven,
The Most Hígh gave fórth His voíce.
15 He sént forth His árrows and scáttered them,
He shót with His líghtnings and "troúbled[1]" them.
16 Then the béd of the wáters was séen,
The foundátions of éarth were laid báre,
At thy chíding O Jáhve—
At the blást of the "bréath of Thy nóstrils[2]."
17 He sént from on hígh, He tóok me,
Dréw me from mány wáters,

---

[1] Ex. xiv. 24.   [2] Ex. xv. 8.

18　Fréed me from énemies míghty,
　　From fóes that were strónger than Í.
19　In that dáy of my wéakness they mét me,
　　But Jáhve becáme my stáy :
20　He broúght me fórth into líberty,
　　He fréed me becaúse He lóves me.

The rhythm in this fine passage is regular except in *vv.* 12, 13, where there is reason to think that the present text is not altogether correct. The Psalm is, of course, a national Psalm and recounts the deliverance of Israel at the Red Sea by that free choice of God which indicates a fuller deliverance in the future (*v.* 20).

CHAPTER III

THE ḲÎNAH

THE origin of the *Ḳînah* is the lament for the dead. We have already seen that, even in the oldest Lament that has come down to us from the times of David, the intensity of grief found a natural expression in the occurrence of short sob-like lines. Thus:

> Thy lóve to mé more márvellous
> Than wóman's lóve!

In later times professional mourners were engaged at funerals and the *Ḳînah* became a distinct measure or rhythm. Thus we read (2 Chron. xxxv. 25): "And Jeremiah *lamented* for Josiah and all the singing men and singing women spake of Josiah in their *Ḳînahs* (i.e. *lamentations*) unto this day."

But since nations die as well as individuals the Prophets often use the *Ḳînah* to lament their death. Even in the earlier Prophets like Amos (*c.* 750 B.C.), we find perfect specimens of the *Ḳînah*, e.g. Amos v. 2:

> She is fállen, to ríse no móre,
> The Vírgin of Ísrael!
> Spread oút upón her lánd,
> Nóne to upráise her!

Compare also Amos viii. 10. The *Ķînah* is frequent in the writings of Jeremiah and in those of Ezekiel.

Thus Jeremiah (ix. 10 ff.) says :

> On the moúntains I táke up a wáiling;
> On the wílderness pástures a Ķínah.
> They are búrned that nóne can pass thróúgh them!
> Nor can soúnd of cáttle be héard!
> From bírd of héaven to béast
>   They are fléd and góne!
> And I máke of Jerúsalem héaps,
>   A dwélling of drágons!
> And the cíties of Júdah I máke desolátion
>   That nóne can inhábit!

And again, in *vv.* 17 ff. :

> Consider ye, and call for the Ķínah-women that they may
>   come...
> Let them táke up a wáiling for ús,
> That our éyes may run óver with wéeping,
>   Our éyelids gush wáter.
> .   .   .   .
> Téach ye your daúghters the dírge ;
> Each óne her neíghbour the Ķínah.
> For Déath is come úp to our wíndows,
> Éntered withín our pálaces!
> Cutting off chíld from the stréet,
>   Yoúths from the márket!

Jeremiah (xxxviii. 22) pictures the women of the royal house of Judah taunting Zedekiah when fallen

into the hands of his quondam allies, the Chaldeans,
and saying :

> They decéived and outmástered thee quíte,
>   These mén of thy péace!
> Thy féet are súnk in the míre,
>   They are túrned away báck !

I believe that Budde (Hast. Dict. *Poetry Hebrew*)
is right in maintaining that the *Ḳînah* was, *par
excellence*, the verse of the women. It was used by
them chiefly as mourners for the dead, but also, as
we have seen, in taunt-songs. The Prophets naturally
express themselves in the language of their day and
frequently use this popular metre, not only as the
genuine expression of sorrow, but also, as the taunt-
song directed against the nations of the world whose
downfall they foresee. Ezekiel constantly mentions
the *Ḳînah* (ii. 10; xix. 1, 14; xxvi. 17; xxvii. 2, 32;
xxviii. 12; xxxii. 2, 16), and uses the metre in his
lament over the deportation of the two princes.

In translating this we must retain the Hebrew
word *k'phír*, which the E.V. generally translates
"*young lion*," since the Hebrew has many words for
"*lion*," the English only one. *K'phír* denotes a lion
that has attained to maturity.

(Ezek. xix. 2 ff.)

> Whát of thy móther the líoness ?
> Amóng *k'phírîm* she noúrished her whélps.

And she broúght up óne of her whélps;
      A *k'phír* he became.
And he léarned to tear préy, | he áte mén.
So the nátions heard rúmour aboút him;
      In their pít he was táken:
To the Lánd of Égypt they broúght him in cháins.
When she sáw she had wáited, | her hópe disappoínted,
She chóse out óne of her whélps
      She máde him *k'phír*:
So he wálked aboút among líons;—
      A *k'phír* he becáme.
And he léarned to tear préy, | he áte mén.
And he knew... [*text doubtful*]
      And their cíties he wásted
Till the Lánd with its fúlness lay désolate
      At the soúnd of his róaring.
So the Nátions set ón him | from próvinces roúnd;
And they spréad out their nét aroúnd him:
      In their pít he was táken:
So they pút him in cáge in cháins,
And broúght him to Bábylon's kíng,
      And broúght him to stróngholds
That his voíce should néver be heard agáin
      On the moúntains of Ísrael.

This passage has all the appearance of having been written in the regular *Ḳinah* measure. I have endeavoured to reproduce the irregularities so that the English reader may judge for himself how far the text may have suffered.

Ezekiel uses the *Ḳinah* in his "Laments" over Tyre (xxvi. 17 ff.; xxvii.; xxviii. 12 ff.) and over

Pharaoh (xxxii. 2 ff.). In all these cases we might
have expected *mashal,* *"parable"* or *"taunt-song,"*
rather than *Ḳinah.* Ezekiel seems to have been
specially fond of the *mashal.* See his parable of the
Great Eagle (xvii. 1—10); of the *seething pot* (xxiv.
3—5) and also of the *mother and daughter* (xvi. 44 f.).
This style of teaching must have been popular with
some (Ezek. xxxiii. 30—32), while others said, with
contempt, *"Is he not a speaker of mashals?"* (xx. 49;
in the Hebrew, xxi. 5).

The style of Ezekiel is somewhat diffuse, but I am
not sure that his real gift as a poet has been appre-
ciated. He was a young man when the mighty
Empire of Assyria fell (606 B.C.) never to rise again.
The battle of Carchemish in the following year
shattered the power of Egypt; and Ezekiel held
up before Pharaoh the warning of Assyria's fall in
a fine poem written in a somewhat irregular *Ḳinah*
measure as follows:

(Ezek. xxxi. 3 ff.)

3　Behóld Asshúr | a cédar in Lébanon | beaúteous in bránches,
　　　shádowy with léafage | and lófty in heíght;
　　And amíd the thick boúghs | his tóp-shoot aróse.
4　Wáters enlárged him | the déep made him grów.
　　It rán with its rívers all roúnd | the pláce of his plánting,
　　And sént forth its líttle canáls | to all trées of the fiéld:
5　Thérefore his státure was hígher | than all trées of the fiéld,
　　And his boúghs became mány | his bránches grew lóng | as
　　　he shót forth from mány waters.

6 In his boúghs there did nést | all bírds of the héaven ;
   And únder his bránches there géndered | all béasts of the
        fiéld ;
   And there dwélt in his shádow | the whóle of the nátions.
7 So he gréw fair in greátness, | in léngth of his bránches | be-
        caúse that his róot reached | to wáters so mány.
8 There eclípsed him no cédars | in Gárden of Gód.
   The fir-trees were nót like his boúghs, | nor were chésnut
        trees líke to his bránches.
   No trée in the Gárden of Gód | could compáre unto hím in
        its béauty.

The latter part of this poem which depicts the
fall of Assyria to Hades is singularly like the *Ḳinah*
poem on the fall of Babylon which we must consider
at greater length.

A fine example of the *Ḳinah* is this taunt-song
(Is. xiv. 4 ff.) written by an unknown poet, *c.* 549 B.C.,
not long before the fall of Babylon.

The text of this poem is well-nigh perfect. The
only change I have suggested is to transpose verses
18, 19.

The natural divisions of the poem occur after
verses 6, 8, 11, 15, 17. There is a progress and
development of thought which might justify us in
speaking of these divisions as strophes. Thus :

Strophe I, *vv.* 4—6.   The fall of Babylon ascribed
                        to Jahve.
Strophe II, *vv.* 7, 8.   The world of nature rejoices.
Strophe III, *vv.* 9—11.   Grim joy in Hades.

Strophe IV, *vv.* 12—15.   The Nations take up the
                              taunt-song.
Strophe V, *vv.* 16, 17.   Hades takes up the taunt.
Strophe VI, *vv.* 19—20.   The Nations conclude
                              with the moral.

Thus strophe VI answers to strophe IV, strophe V
to strophe III, while strophes I and II form a general
introduction.   The portion of the poem referring to
Hades is worthy of Dante.   We see the King of
Terrors rousing up the shades from their shadowy
thrones to greet the latest failure of earth's ambitions.
We note also the "narrow" look with which the newly
awakened shades regard him, as though unable to
trust their eyesight (*v.* 16).

(Is. xiv. 4 ff.)

4   Thou shalt take up this proverb (i.e. taunt-song) against the
      King of Babylon and thou shalt say:

STROPHE I.

Áh! the Tásk-master nów is at rést!
      The Góld-city (?) résteth!
5   Jáhve hath bróken the stáff of the wícked ;
      The scéptre of rúlers ;
6   That smóte the Péoples in wráth ;
      With céaseless smíting.
That rúled the Nátions in ánger ;
      With unspáring pursúit.

Strophe II.

7 All éarth is at rést and is quíet;
      They búrst into sóng!
8 The fír-trees themsélves rejoíce over thée;
      The cédars of Lébanon;
No héwer hath cóme up agáinst us,
      Since thoú art laid dówn.

Strophe III.

9 Hádes belów is in túmult for thée;
      To wélcome thy cóming;
For thée it aroúseth the shádes;
      All the hé-goats of éarth.
It máketh to ríse from their thrónes,
      All the kíngs of the Nátions.
10 [*They áll of them ánswer and sáy unto thée*]
So thoú too art wéakened as wé,
      Made líke unto ús?
11 Thy príde is brought dówn unto Hádes;
      The thrúm of thy víols.
Benéath thee corrúption is stréwn:
      And the wórm is thy cóver.

Strophe IV.

12 Hów art thou fállen from Héaven,
      Thou Stár of the Dáwn!
(Hów art thou) héwn to the groúnd,
      That didst wéaken the Nátions!
13 Thoú, that didst sáy in thine heárt,
      I will moúnt unto Héaven.
Abóve the stárs of Gód
      I will sét up my thróne;

And will sít in the Moúnt of Assémbly[1];
  The Recéss of the Nórth.
14 I will moúnt on the heíghts of the cloúds;
  Will be líke the Most Hígh.
15 Yet to Hádes it ís thou art broúght
  The Recéss of the Pit.

STROPHE V.

16 They that sée thee look nárrowly ón thee;
  Upón thee they pónder.
Is thís the mán that troúbled éarth,
  That shóok the kíngdoms?
17 That máde the wórld a wílderness,
  Its cíties wásted?
That néver freed prísoner hómeward!

STROPHE VI.

19 And thoú art cast fórth from thy gráve,
  As a shóot that's rejécted!
Clóthed with the mángled sláin, that go dówn to the stónes
  of the Pít,
  As a cárcass that's trámpled.
18 One and áll, the kíngs of the Nátions,
Líe down in hónour, éach in his hoúse.
20 Not with thém art thou joíned in thy búrial;
Sínce thy lánd thou destróyedst,
  Thy péople didst sláy.
Unhónoured for éver remaíneth
  The séed of ill-dóers.

The dirge of the captives (Ps. cxxxvii.) is, as we
might expect, written for the most part in the *Ḵînah*
measure. The text is a little uncertain in *v.* 3[b] where,

[1] i.e. of the gods.

also, the metre fails us. We are glad to feel that *vv.* 7—9 were not written by the author of this lovely Psalm which is complete in itself (*vv.* 1—6). The reader should notice how the word *"joy"* in *v.* 6ᵇ responds to *"joy"* in *v.* 3ᵇ. Any personal joy was impossible when Jerusalem was in ruins. Verse 6ᵃ responds to *v.* 3ᵃ. The voice of song would, if attempted, mean that "the tongue would cleave to the palate." Verse 5 responds to *v.* 2. Should the harp be taken down the right hand itself would refuse its office.

Thus the parallelism of thought completes itself in two strophes.

(Ps. cxxxvii.)

1   By Bábylon's wáters we sát, and we wépt,
         As we thóught upon Zíon.

2   Thére on the wíllows withín her
         We hánged our hárps.

3   For thére our cáptors demánded
         The lánguage of sóng!
   Our wásters (?)...(asked) jóy!
   "Síng us óne of Zíon's Sóngs."

4   Hów should we síng the Sóng of Jáhve
         On Lánd of strángers?

5   Could Í forget thée O Jerúsalem
         My right hánd should forgét!

6   My tóngue should cléave to my pálate
         If unmíndful of thée!
   If I sét not Jerúsalem hígher
         Than bést of my jóy.

Before leaving the *Ḳinah* we will give an illustration of the way in which it is occasionally modified. The reader will note the grief expressed by the short lines.

(Is. i. 21 ff.)

Hów is she túrned to a hárlot!
　　　　The fáithful Cíty!
Fúll (she was) of jústice, | ríghteousness dwelt ín her—
　　　　But nów—assássins!
Thy sílver is cóme to be dróss; | Thy wíne is múrdered with
　　wáter;
Thy nóbles are rébels; | Compánions of thiéves:
Each óne of them lóveth the bríbe, | And pursúeth the gíft.
The órphan they júdge not; | the caúse of the wídow | comes
　　nót unto thém!

These examples may suffice, especially as we shall have occasion to consider at some length the *Ḳinah* measure in the Book of Lamentations in our chapter which treats of Alphabetical Poetry.

It may be well, however, to give one example of the way in which the study of Hebrew metre may eventually help us to determine the original text. For this purpose I take Ps. xlii., xliii., which is in the *Ḳinah* measure with a refrain in the measure 3 + 3. This Psalm has been carefully analysed by Prof. Rothstein (*Grundzüge des hebräischen Rhythmus*), and I shall to some extent follow his analysis, though my conclusions differ from his.

K.   4

The first line (*v.* 2) is in different measure (viz. $2 + 2 + 2 + 2$). The question therefore arises: Is it intended as a heading for the Psalm? I have retained the word "*bleateth*" because the Hebrew word is onomatopoetic, denoting the voice of the thirsty stag. We have no word in English for this. But the English reader has a right to know that the Poet applies this strong word to the cry of his soul.

As bléateth the stág | for the chánnels of wáters, | so bléateth my sóul | for Thée, O Gód.

It is obvious that, in this line of four parts, the *third* answers exactly to the *first*, and the *fourth* to the *second*. I therefore suggest that, if it be the heading of the whole Psalm, it should imply *four strophes answering to one another in this order*.

Our next step must be to omit *vv.* 5, 9 and *vv.* 1, 2ᵃ of Ps. xliii. which read as prose ; also xliii. 2ᵇ which is a repetition of xlii. 10ᵇ.

With these omissions the Psalm falls into four equal strophes which answer to one another in the order suggested by the heading.   Thus :

(Ps. xlii.—xliii.)

2   As bléateth the stág | for the chánnels of wáters, | so
       bléateth my sóul | for Thée, O Gód |

STROPHE I ("*As bleateth the stag*").   Scheme $3+2$: Refrain $3+3$.

3   My sóul is athírst for Jáhve—
             For the Gód of my lífe !

　　　Whén shall I cóme and behóld
　　　　　The Présence of Jáhve?
4　Téars have been míne for fóod,
　　　　　By dáy and by níght,
　　While they sáy to me áll day lóng,
　　　　　Whére is thy Gód?

Refrain.

6　Whý so deprésed, O my sóul?
　　And whý shouldst thou móan withín me?
　　Wáit for Jáhve till I thánk Him,
　　As the hélp of my fáce, and my Gód.

STROPHE II ("*For the channels of waters*").

7　Withín me my sóul is cast dówn,
　　　　　Since I célebrate Thée
　　From a Lánd of Jórdan and Hérmons—
　　　　　A moúntain of Mítzor!
8　Where déep is crýing to déep,
　　　　　For the soúnd of Thy tórrents!
　　The whóle of Thy breákers and bíllows
　　　　　Have góne over mé.

　　　　　(*Repeat Refrain.*)

STROPHE III ("*So bleateth my soul*").

10　I would sáy to the Gód of my Róck,
　　　　　Why shoúldst Thou forgét me?
　　Whý should I moúrnfully wálk
　　　　　Through oppréssion of fóes?
11　'Tis as múrder withín my bónes
　　　　　When mine énemies revíle me;
　　When they sáy to me áll day lóng
　　　　　Whére is thy Gód?
12　　　　　(*Repeat Refrain.*)

STROPHE IV ("*For Thee, O God*").

(Ps. xliii.)

3   Sénd forth Thy Líght and Thy Trúth;
          Let thém lead me ón:
     To Thy hóly Moúnt let them bríng me—
          Únto Thy Tábernacles.
4   Till I cóme to the Áltar of Jáhve—
          To the Gód of my jóy;
     And I gléefully thánk Thee with hárp,
          O Jáhve my Gód!
5   (*Repeat Refrain.*)

The Psalm cannot be understood without reference to Joel i. 20 and Job vi. 15—20, for it is not the *thirst* of the stag but the *disappointed* thirst when it finds the channel dry. So, also it is not the *thirst* of the soul but the *disappointed* thirst when the channels of grace yield no joy (strophes II and III). But the refrain insists upon the truth that these channels of grace will again flow with joy, and the fourth strophe sees the realization of this hope.

The passage in Joel to which we refer may be translated as follows:

(Joel i. 19 f.)

Jáhve to Thée I crý—
For fíre hath devoúred the pástures of the wílderness;
And fláme hath enkíndled all the trées of the fiéld.
The béasts of the fiéld are each bléating unto Thée.
For dríed are the chánnels of wáter;
And fire hath devoúred the pástures of the wílderness.

Though the regular form of the *Ḳinah* is 3 + 2 we have already seen that it admits of modifications. One further instance may be given from the beautiful elegy on Moab (Is. xvi. 9 ff.) which Isaiah seems to have quoted from an ancient source (see *v.* 13).

To understand this elegy the reader must remember that the word *hēdad* which properly signifies the joyous *"vintage-shout"* may also signify the *"battle-shout,"* so that Jeremiah (xlviii. 33) speaks of a "hēdad that is no hēdad." In our elegy the word is used in both senses.

The metre is 2 + 2 + 2 with two lines of 2 + 2 + 2 + 2.

Thérefore I wéep | with the wéeping of Jázer | for Síbmah's
    víne.
I bedéw thee with téars | Heshbón El'áléh | for on hárvest and
    frúitage | the *hĕdad* is fállen !
Góne is all gládness | and jóy from the tíllage | the víneyards
    are sóngless, | not rínging with shoút.
The wíne in the présses | no tréader now tréads ; | the *hĕdad*
    is sílenced !
So my bówels for Móab | are soúnding as hárps, | and my
    sóul for Kir-héres.

There is a play upon the name " *Kir-heres,*" as in Is. xix. 18 ; the *"City of the Sun,"* is become the *" City of destruction."* The whole passage also contains instances of alliteration of which Isaiah was peculiarly fond and which it is impossible to reproduce in a translation.

CHAPTER IV

ACROSTIC, OR ALPHABETICAL, POETRY

THE poems in the Bible which are directly alphabetical are the following : Pss. ix. and x. (imperfect), xxv., xxxiv., xxxvii., cxi., cxii., cxix., cxlv. ; Prov. xxxi. 10—31; Lam. i., ii., iii., iv.   At first sight the arrangement of lines or verses under the order of successive letters of the alphabet might seem beneath the dignity of the Sacred Writings.   Nor is it sufficient to regard such arrangement as an aid to memory.   I hope to shew that it had a deeper significance, and that it indicates a division in strophes which has not yet been recognised.

The Book of Lamentations consists of five chapters. These chapters are of different date and of different structure.   The first chapter is generally recognised to be the oldest ; each verse consists of three lines, the first line of each verse commencing with the corresponding letter of the alphabet.   The metre is elegiac, i.e. *Ḳinah* measure, the poem being a lament over the death of Israel as a Nation.

We give a translation of the first two verses as a specimen:

(Lam. i. 1 f.)

א Hów doth she sít all alóne |
          the (once) pópulous Cíty !
Hów hath she cóme to be wídowed |
          once greát among nátions !
Shé that was quéen among kíngdoms |
          now cóme under tríbute !

ב She bítterly wéeps in the níght |
          with her téars on her chéek !
She háth not a óne to bring cómfort |
          out of áll of her lóvers !
Her friénds are turned tráitors towárds her |
          they have cóme to be énemies !

The second chapter is similar to the first except for the fact that the order of two of the letters (פ and ע) is transposed. The third chapter is supposed to be the latest. It has three lines to each letter of the alphabet; a verse has been assigned to each letter, thus giving 66 verses though, properly, there should have been only 22. *Here again we note that the letter* פ (*vv.* 46—48) *comes before the letter* ע (*vv.* 49—51), and this is the case also in the fourth chapter. We begin to suspect that this represents the original order of the Hebrew alphabet; we therefore turn back to chapter I and we find that *vv.* 16 and 17 which represent ע and פ respectively would give better sense if transposed. We are thus confirmed in our belief that, at the time when these chapters of Lamentations were composed, the order of the letters was פ, ע, not ע, פ as at present. We shall see the importance of this when we come to the earlier group of Alphabetical Psalms. Chapters IV and V have two lines to a verse but chapter V differs in that it is not alphabetical, and the lines are shorter.

Thus the Book of Lamentations consists of five Elegies, the oldest of which may date almost from the age of Jeremiah. These elegies were appointed for use on the 9th of Ab when the Jewish Church bewailed the destruction of the first Temple. I suggest that they were composed, at different dates, for use on that Fast-day.

We will now translate Lam. iii. retaining as far as possible the rhythm of the Hebrew.

(Lam. iii.)

1 א I am the mán that hath lóoked on afflíction—
by the ród of His wráth.

2 א He léd me and máde me to wálk
in dárkness, not líght.

3 א Agáinst me He cónstantly túrneth His hánd—
áll the dáy.

4 ב He hath wórn out my flésh and my skín—
bróken my bónes.

5 ב He hath buílded and cómpassed me roúnd—
with gáll and with trávail.

6 ב He hath máde me to dwéll in dark pláces—
   as the áge-long déad.

7 ג He hath hédged me aroúnd, that I cánnot go fórth[1]—
   He hath weíghted my cháin.

8 ג Yeá, though I crý out and shoút—
   He shúts out my práyer.

9 ג He hath hédged my wáys (as with) héwn-stone—
   He hath twísted my páths.

10 ד He ís to mé as a beár in wáit—
   as a líon[2] in cóverts.

11 ד My wáys He hath túrned, He hath púlled me in piéces—
   hath réndered me désolate.

12 ד He bént His bów, and He sét me
   as the márk for the árrow[3].

13 ה He hath caúsed to énter my réins
   the sháfts of His qúiver.

14 ה I becáme a derísion to áll the Péoples—
   their sóng all the dáy.

15 ה He hath fílled me with bítterness, máde me
   drúnken with wórmwood.

16 ו And He bráke my téeth with grável—
   féd (?) me with áshes.

17 ו Thou hast cást out my sóul from péace—
   I forgát (all) prospérity.

18 ו And I sáid, my glóry hath pérished—
   and my hópe all from Jáhve.

19 ז I remémber my afflíction and my sórrow—
   wórmwood and gáll.

[1] Cf. Job xix. 8, xxx. 20.   [2] Job x. 16.
[3] Cf. Job vii. 20, xvi. 12 f.

20 ז My sóul hath them stíll in remémbrance—
                    is húmbled withín me!

21 ז This óne thing I láy to my heárt—
                    thérefore I hópe.

Israel trusts in the Covenant of Creation (Jer. xxxi. 35—37 ; Is. lxvi. 22).

22 ח Jáhve's mércies are not énded[1]—
                    His compássions fáil not.

23 ח They are néw as the mórnings come roúnd—
                    Greát is Thy fáithfulness.

24 ח My pórtion is Jáhve, saith my sóul—
                    I thérefore awáit Him.

25 ט Góod to His pátient ones is Jáhve—
                    to the sóul that doth séek Him.

26 ט Góod, one should hópe and be stíll—
                    for salvátion of Jáhve.

27 ט Góod, for mán that he should beár—
                    the yóke in his youth.

28 י Let him sít alóne and be sílent—
                    since He láid it upón him.

29 י Let him pút his moúth in the dúst—
                    if perchánce there be hópe.

30 י Let him gíve his chéek to the smíter[2]—
                    be fílled with repróach.

31 כ For He wíll not cast óff for éver—
                    the Lord (will be gracious).

32 כ For thóugh He cause griéf He will píty—
                    as His mércy aboúnds.

---

[1] See Versions.   [2] Is. l. 6.

33 כ For 'tis nót from His heárt He afflícteth
           or griéveth mankind.
34 ל That hé (the enemy) should crúsh under fóot
           all the boúnd ones of éarth—
35 ל That hé should pervért human jústice
           in the fáce of the Híghest—
36 ל That he wróng a mán in his cóvenant—
           The Lórd cannot sée!

37 מ Who ís there that spáke and it wás—
           if the Lórd did not órder?
38 מ Shoúld there not cóme from the moúth of the Híghest—
           Évil and góod?
39 מ What is mán that líveth, to múrmur?—
           a mán for his síns?

40 נ Let us séarch and try our wáys—
           and retúrn unto Jáhve.
41 נ Let us líft our heárts, palms uplífted,—
           to Gód in the Héavens.
42 נ It is wé that transgréssed and rebélled
           and Thoú hast not párdoned!

43 ס Thou hast hédged Thee with ánger and fóllowed us hárd—
           Thou hast sláin without píty.
44 ס Thou hast hédged Thee aroúnd with thick cloúd—
           that práyer cannot páss.
45 ס Thou hast máde us as dróss and as réfuse—
           in the mídst of the Péoples.

46 פ They gápe on us ópen moúthed—
           even áll our énemies.
47 פ Féar and snáre are oúrs—
           desolátion, destrúction.

48 פ Mine éye runs foúntains of wáters—
                    for the húrt of my Péople.

49 ע Mine éye runs dówn and céaseth not—
                    with nó intermíssion.
50 ע Till Hé look fórth and behóld—
                    Even Jáhve from Héaven.
51 ע Mine éye afférteth my sóul—
                    for the daúghters of my Cíty.

52 צ They húnted me sóre like a bírd—
                    my caúseless énemies.
53 צ They cút off my lífe in the dúngeon—
                    and pláced a stone ón me.
54 צ Wáters flowed óver mine héad—
                    I sáid, I am énded.

55 ק I cálled Thy Náme, O Jáhve—
                    from the dépths of the dúngeon.
56 ק My voíce Thou hast héard, Oh clóse not Thine éar—
                    from my bréathing, my crý.
57 ק Thou wast néar in the dáy that I cálled Thee—
                    Thou sáidest, Fear nót.

58 ר Lórd, Thou hast pléaded the caúse of my sóul—
                    hast ránsomed my lífe.
59 ר Thou, Jáhve, hast wítnessed my wrónging—
                    gíve me now jústice !
60 ר Thou hast séen all their véngeance—
                    their devísings agáinst me.

61 ש Thou hast héard their repróach, O Jáhve—
                    their devíce all agáinst me.
62 ש The tálk and the thoúght of mine ádversaries—
                    agáinst me all dáy.

63 ש Behóld! when they sít, when they ríse—
I am their sóng.

64 ת Rénder them their récompense, O Jáhve—
like the wórk of their hánds.

65 ת Gíve to them blíndness of heárt—
Thy cúrse upón them.

66 ת Pursúe them in wráth and destróy them—
from benéath Jahve's héavens.

At first sight this poem seems to consist of alternations of sorrow and hope without order or arrangement: but if we look closer we find that the natural breaks occur after the letters ו, ל, צ, ת. This gives three long strophes of 6 letters each closed by a short strophe of 4 letters. In other words, the *arrangement of the strophes corresponds with the law of the Ḳinah measure* (3 + 2), *in which the poem is written*. This, of course, may be accidental. We shall test it further. Meanwhile it is suggestive. The subjects of the four strophes may be given as follows:

Strophe I (6 letters א to ו). *Complaint against God.*

Strophe II (6 letters ז to ל). *Resignation and hope.*

Strophe III (6 letters מ to צ). *Complaint against God modified by resignation.*

Strophe IV (4 letters ק to ת). *God   has   heard,
and will repay
the enemy.*

If we name these strophes A, B, C, D, respectively,
then, if the poem be studied, it will be seen that
C answers to A and D to B.   Besides this larger
division into strophes the reader will notice that *the
letter מ has become the middle letter of the alphabet.*
He should therefore compare the three א lines with
the three מ lines and so throughout the alphabet.
This will throw great light on the poem.   Note
especially the relation between א and מ (*vv.* 1—3
with 37—39).

> ג and ס (*vv.* 7—9 with 43—45).

> ר and פ (*vv.* 10—12 with 46—48).

> ו and צ (*vv.* 16—18 with 52—54).

The *six* letters ז to ל (*vv.* 19—36) have to correspond with the *four* letters ק to ת (*vv.* 55—66).
It should be noted especially how *vv.* 34—36 are
answered by the curse in *vv.* 64—66.

We will now test our conclusions by seeing how
far they apply to the Alphabetical Psalms.   For this
purpose we choose Ps. xxxvii. as being one of the
most perfect specimens of the Alphabetical Psalms of
the First Collection.

(Ps. xxxvii.   Scheme 3 + 3.)

Strophe I.

1   א   Frét not thysélf at ill-dóers, | Grúdge not at wórkers of
        wróng.

2   For as gráss they are spéedily mówn, | And líke the
        green hérbage they wíther.

3   ב   Trúst in Jáhve and do góod ; | Dwéll in the Land, féed
        on His Fáith.

4   And delíght thee in Jáhve, | that Hé may grant thée |
        the desíre of thy heárt.

5   ג   Devólve upon Jáhve thy wáy ; | Trúst Him, and Hé will
        dó it.

·6   He will bríng out thy ríght as the líght, | And thy
        caúse as the nóonday.

7   ד   Be stíll for Jáhve ; wáit for Him !—
        Frét not at hím that próspers, | At the mán that effécts
        his desígns.

8   ה   Céase from ánger; leave wráth; | Frét not; 'tis mérely
        for hárm.

9   For íll-doers sháll be cut óff, | While the wáiters on
        Jáhve are théy | that inhérit the Lánd.

10 ⌈ ו   Yet but a líttle and the wícked is nót ! | Thou may'st ⌉
    | pónder his pláce, but he ís not! |
    | While the húmble inhérit the Lánd | And delíght in |
    ⌊   abúndance of péace.   ⌋

Strophe II.

12 ז   The wícked laid pláns for the ríghteous, | And gnáshed
        at hím with his téeth.

13   The Lórd will laúgh at hím, | For He sées that his dáy is
        cóming.

14   ח   The wícked have dráwn their swórd, | Have bént their
         bów—
         To cást down the póor and néedy, | To slaúghter those
         úpright of wáy.
15   Their swórd shall piérce thine own heárt | And their
         bóws shall be bróken.

16   ט   A ríghteous man's líttle is bétter, | Than abúndance of
         mány wícked.
17   For the árms of the wícked shall be bróken, | While
         Jáhve uphóldeth the ríghteous.

18   י   Jáhve nóteth the dáys of the úpright, | So their héritage
         lásts for éver.
19   They áre not shámed in evil tímes, | And in dáys of
         déarth they are fílled.

20   כ   But wícked-ones pérish—
         And Jáhve's enemies, | like the béauty of the méadows, |
         Are pást in smóke and góne.

21   ל   The wícked bórroweth and páyeth nót; | While the
         ríghteous is grácious and gíving.
         For His bléssed inhérit the Lánd; | His cúrsed ones
         áre cut óff.

STROPHE III.

23   מ   'Tis from Jáhve the stéps of a mán are estáblished, |
         When his wáy gives Him pléasure.
24   Though he fáll he will nót be cast óff, | For Jáhve up-
         hóldeth his hánd.

25   נ   Yoúng I wás and now am óld | Yet never sáw the
         ríghteous léft | [Or his séed bégging bréad…] ?gloss.
26   He is éver grácious and léndeth; | And his séed is for
         bléssing.

27 ס Túrn from évil and dó the góod, | And dwéll thou for
éver.

28 For Jáhve lóveth jústice, | And will néver desért His
sáints.

30 פ The moúth of the ríghteous méditates wisdom, | And
his tóngue will be tálking of júdgement.

31 In his heárt is the Láw of his Gód, | So his stéps do not
fálter.

28ᵇ ע Sínners are destroyed [? *text*]... | The séed of the wícked
is cut óff.
The ríghteous inhérit the Lánd, | And dwéll thereín
for éver.

The structure of the poem requires that פ should
come before ע just as it does in Lamentations. I have
therefore transposed these lines.

STROPHE IV.

32 צ The wícked sets wátch for the ríghteous, | And séeketh
to sláy him—

33 Jáhve will not léave him in his hánd, | Nor condémn
him when júdged—

34 ק Wáit thou for Jáhve and kéep His Wáy, | To inhérit the
Lánd will He ráise thee.
Thou shalt jóy in the wícked's extínction.

35 ר I have séen the wícked tyránnically stróng, | Outspréading
as Lébanon cédars.

36 I pássed—and ló, he was góne ; | I soúght him—he
coúld not be foúnd !

37 ש Nóte the pérfect (man), regárd the úpright, | For the
mán of péace has a fúture :

38   While transgréssors are whólly destróyed ; | The fúture of
            the wícked is extínct.

39   ת   The salvátion of the ríghteous is from Jáhve, | Their
            strónghold in tíme of distréss.

40   For 'tis Jáhve that hélps and delívers them; | Delívers
            from sínners and sáves them, | Becaúse they confíded
            in Hím.

The structure of this Alphabetical Psalm is in
short lines of 3 beats, but it is better to arrange it in
longer lines of 6 beats with cæsura, for the most part,
in the middle. The reason for this will be seen in
vv. 4, 7ª, 20, 34ᵇ, 40, where the arrangement is varied.
The letters of the alphabet are divided into four
groups, with the letter מ as the middle letter, exactly
as in Lam. iii., so that the Psalm falls into four corresponding strophes. But whereas in Lam. iii., where
the *Ḳinah* measure was 3 + 2, we had three long
strophes and one short one, here, where the measure
is 3 + 3 the strophes are of equal length of 5 letters
each. But, since there are 22 letters in the Hebrew
alphabet, and the letter מ must always be the central
letter, the author of our Psalm had two superfluous
letters in the first half, i.e. the letters ו and ל at the
end of strophes I and II. He might have omitted
these letters altogether, as did the original author
of Pss. xxv. and xxxiv. (see my notes), in which case
they would probably have been supplied by a later
editor ; or he might himself have written these

verses (10 and 21) with the intention of adding no
new thought.

In my opinion the concluding lines of *vv.* 9, 20,
which remind us of alexandrines, formed the original
close of strophes I and II respectively ; I have
therefore placed *vv.* 10, 21 in square brackets. The
reader should now carefully compare the four
strophes, not regarding the *verses* (which have no
ancient authority), but the *Hebrew letters.* He will
see that the closest relationship is between the five
letters of strophe I and those of strophe III, and
also between the five letters of strophe II and those
of strophe IV. Thus the relationship of the strophes
is identical with that of Lam. iii.

The main subject of the Psalm is the religious
difficulty caused by the prosperity of the wicked.
The subject of strophe I (see esp. *vv.* 5, 6) is the
command *to cast the burden of this difficulty upon
God.* Strophe III answers, letter by letter, to
strophe I but adds the thought of active work (cf.
esp. *vv.* 27, 28 with *vv.* 5, 6).

Strophe II, in its central thought (*v.* 16), asserts
that in spite of the poverty and low estate of the
righteous, their condition is better than that of their
triumphant enemies. Strophe IV takes up this
thought of strophe II, letter by letter, and comes to
the conclusion, which, as we shall see, did not satisfy
Job, that a sudden destruction which will overtake

the wicked (*vv.* 35, 36) will justify the ways of God with men.

Before leaving the subject of Alphabetical poetry, we must take one example from the Psalms of the Third Collection, which we naturally expect to be of later date than the poems we have already considered. We select the pair of Psalms cxi. and cxii. which, indeed, form one Psalm in two strophes.

(Ps. cxi.)

Scheme 3 + 3.   Subject, *The Good God.*

א Jáhve I práise with whole heárt, | ב In commúnion of sáints and assémbly.

ג Greát are the wórks of Jáhve; | ד Éxquisite to áll that chóose them.

ה Spléndour and májesty is His wórk; | ו His ríghteousness abídeth for éver.

ז A Náme hath He máde by His wónders; | ח "Grácious and Mérciful" is Jáhve.

ט He gíveth fóod to his féarers; | י He remémbereth His Cóvenant for éver.

כ His pówer He shéwed for His Péople; | ל Gíving them the héritage of Géntiles.

מ The wórks of His hánds are vérity; | נ Áll of his précepts are súre.

ס They are stáyed for éver and éver; | ע Being wroúght in trúth and ríght.

פ Redémption He sént to His Péople; | צ He enjoíned His Cóvenant for éver.

ק Hóly and féared is His Náme.

ר   The begínning of wísdom is [Jáhve's] féar ; | ע Discrétion is
theírs that práctise it.

      ת His práise abídeth for éver.

(Ps. cxii.)

Scheme 3 + 3. Subject, *The Good Man.*

א O háppy the féarer of Jáhve, | ב That greátly delíghts in
His Láws.

ג Míghty on éarth is his séed; | ד The generátion of sáints
shall be bléssed.

ה Ríches and wéalth in his hoúse; | ו His ríghteousness
abídeth for éver.

ז His líght is rísen in dárkness; | ח "Grácious and mérciful"
is the ríghteous.

ט He is góod grácious and gíving; | י He maintáineth his
prómises ríghtly.

כ He remáineth unmóved for ever; | ל He shall bé for an
éndless Náme.

מ At évil tídings he feareth nót; | נ Fíxed is his heárt upon
Jáhve.

ס Stáyed is his heárt, unféaring ; | ע Till he sée his desíre on
his fóes.

פ He scáttered, he gáve to the néedy; | צ His ríghteousness
abídeth for éver.

      ק His hórn is exálted with hónour.

ר The wícked sées and is griéved ; | ש He gnásheth his téeth
and píneth.

      ת The desíre of wícked (men) périshes.

Each of these Psalms is complete in itself. Each
is divided into two Parts or strophes at the letter מ,

as in the case of other alphabetical arrangements.
Thus, if we analyse Ps. cxi. we see that in Part I
the central thought is *the Covenant Name of God*
as "*Gracious and Merciful*" in letters ו, ח. If we
refer to the corresponding line in Part II we see
that it reads, under letter ק, "*Holy and feared is
His Name.*" Indeed the six lines (12 letters) of
Part I correspond with the six lines (10 letters) of
Part II. The same is true of Ps. cxii. which speaks
of the *good man*. The central thought of Part I is
given by the letters ו, ח viz. that, out of his darkness,
a *light springs up for him* because he *is gracious
and merciful*. The corresponding line in Part II is
given by the letter ק "*His horn is exalted with
honour.*" The connexion in Hebrew between the *horn*
and rising *light* may be seen from Ps. cxxxii. 17 f.;
Ex. xxxiv. 29 f., 35; Hab. iii. 4.

If, in each of these Psalms, the reader will carefully
compare Part I with Part II, line by line, he will see
that these Parts are really strophes; so that they
ought to be sung antiphonally. But though each
Psalm is complete in itself the full meaning is only
brought out when we read the two Psalms together,
line by line. The *good man* (Ps. cxii.) is a reflex of
the *Good God* (Ps. cxi.), so much so that the same
words may be applied to each (see letters ו, ח, י).
The liberality of God (Ps. cxi. letters פ, צ) is shewn
in that gift of Redemption which makes His Covenant

eternal. The liberality of the good man (Ps. cxii., letters פ, צ) is shewn in gifts of mercy which make his righteousness eternal (cf. 2 Cor. ix. 9 ff.). Thus, while each Psalm has two strophes, the two Psalms are strophical the one to the other, and should always be sung together.

We may now sum up the results at which we have arrived in our study of the alphabetical poems. In every case the alphabet has been divided at the letter מ, thus giving a grouping of *ten* letters, *ten* being the sacred number of the Priest Code and of the *Covenant*. The allusions to the Covenant in these poems is very frequent. They all belong to the "Wisdom" literature and are didactic in their tone. In the earlier alphabetical poems (Lam. and Pss. of First Collection) the letter פ came before ע. In the later poems (Pss. of Third Collection) the order of the alphabet was as at present.

Since the Hebrew alphabet has 22 letters it is evident that the letter מ, which is the 13th letter cannot be the "middle letter," and yet we find that it was so reckoned by Talmudic writers who thus make the first (א), middle (מ), and last letter (ת) of the alphabet (which in Hebrew spell the word "*truth*") to stand for "*the Seal of God*" (Jerus. Tal. *Sanh.* I. Quoted by Buxtorf, s.v. אמת). This I believe has never been explained. I suggest that the solution is to be found in the arrangement of the Alphabetical

(Covenant) Psalms which we have already considered.

The latest of the alphabetical poems in the Bible is the poem on the "good wife" (Prov. xxxi. 10—31) which probably belongs to the Greek period. It consists of 22 lines, each commencing with the corresponding letter of the Hebrew Alphabet, but it is not divided at the letter מ. It is not easy to see any law on which it is constructed, except that the two last lines sum up the moral, in the nature of a Chorus, thus making the poem itself consist of 20 lines, or two tens, closing with the lines ק, ר which certainly seem to correspond with the opening lines of the poem.

(Prov. xxxi. 10—31.)

א　Whó can attáin a brave wífe ? | Príceless she ís beyond rúbies.

ב　Her húsband's heárt may trúst her | and láck no mánner of gáin.

ג　She requítes him ónly with góod, | áll the dáys of her lífe.

ד　She séeks out wóol and fláx | and wórks with wílling hands.

ה　She is líke the shíps of the tráder, | she bríngeth her fóod from afár.

ו　She ríses while yét it is níght | and supplíeth the néeds of her hóme[1].

ז　She consíders a fiéld and búys it : | with the frúit of her hánds it is plánted[2].

[1] A probable gloss adds " and a law for her maidens."

[2] The text has "she planteth a vineyard." This destroys the metre.

ח　She gírdeth her loíns with míght, | and máketh stróng her árms.

ט　She percéiveth her tráffic succéed ; | her lámp is unquénched by níght.

י　She láyeth her hánds to the spíndle | and her pálms hold the dístaff.

כ　She ópeneth her pálms to the póor | and strétcheth out hands to the néedy.

ל　No féar of the snów for her hoúsehold | for her hoúsehold is doúble-clád.

מ　She máketh her tápestry-cóverings ; | her clóthing fine-línen and púrple.

נ　Her húsband is knówn in the gátes ; | where he sítteth with the élders of the lánd.

ס　She wórketh gárments and sélleth ; | and gírdles she gíves to the mérchant.

ע　So stróng so fíne her clóthing | she laúghs at cóming tíme.

פ　She opéneth her moúth with wísdom, | with kíndly lóre on her tóngue.

צ　She looks wéll to the wáys of her hoúse | and éats no bréad of ídleness.

ק　Her sóns rise úp and bléss her, | and her húsband práises her (sáying)

ר　"Mány daúghters are bráve | but thoú hast excélled them all."

Chorus speaks.

ש　Gráce and beaúty are fléeting and váin, | a Gód-fearing wífe is the óne to be práised.

ת　Gíve her the frúit of her hánds, | while her déeds tell her práise in the gates.

CHAPTER V

THE PROBLEM OF SUFFERING

THE religion of the Jew was an historical religion. It was wrought out, little by little (Heb. i. 1), in the experiences of the Nation. And certainly there never has been a Nation upon earth that might more fitly be termed "the Suffering Nation." But it is equally true to say that there never has been a Nation that has had throughout its history the same consciousness of a Divine call, of a Divine sonship. The problem that Israel had—I do not say to solve, but—to set forth before the world, was how to reconcile the truth of Israel's sonship with the fact of Israel's sufferings.

From the time when Amos (c. 760 B.C.) uttered his noble paradox (Amos iii. 2), down to the time of Christ, the poets and prophets of Israel have striven in divers ways to face the problem, Why should the righteous suffer? In the present Chapter we shall consider some of the attempts that have been made to solve this problem.

But it is impossible to do this until the English reader shall come to realise that modern individuality must not be read into the Psalter, where the speaker is Israel and where "I" and "we" may constantly interchange as in Num. xx. 19 f. "And the children of Israel said unto him (Edom), We will go up by the high way : and if we drink of thy water, I and my cattle, then will I give the price thereof : let me only, without (doing) anything (else), pass through on my feet. And he said, Thou shalt not pass through. And Edom came out against him...." This characteristic of Hebrew thought has, under God's Providence, served a great end, and it is most unfortunate that it should be so constantly disregarded, even by theologians.

We must now briefly review, as far as possible in historical order, the various answers which have been given to the question, Why should the righteous Nation suffer ?

Deuteronomy (622 B.C.) appears to promise to Israel every kind of temporal prosperity. "In the event of obedience, Israel will be 'set on high' above all nations (xxvi. 19, xxviii. 1), and enjoy material superiority over them" (xv. 6^b, xxviii. 12^b, 13). [Driver, *Deuteronomy*, p. 33.]

The School of Deuteronomy expresses itself in such language as that of the Alphabetical Psalms, e.g. Ps. xxxvii. 25 :

> I have been young and now am old,
> Yet never saw the righteous left,
> Or his seed begging bread.

This teaching of course involves an eternal truth, but it might easily become misleading, and was soon found to need supplementing.

The death of good king Josiah in the battle of Megiddo (609 B.C.) and the times that followed gave true men cause to think. Then it was (*c.* 600 B.C.) that Habakkuk pleaded his difficulty with God (Hab. i. 13): "Thou that art of purer eyes than to behold evil, and that canst not look upon wrong, how is it Thou canst look upon the treacherous-ones and holdest Thy peace when the wicked-one (i.e. the Chaldean) swalloweth up the man that is more righteous than he (i.e. Israel)?" Habakkuk found no answer to his difficulty except to trust and wait (Hab. ii. 1—4).

The life-task of Jeremiah (626—586 B.C.), the man of sorrows, was to prove from his own experience, that suffering was a way of service, and did *not* imply the anger of God. His own deep consciousness of sin and infirmity never hid from him the certainty that God had called him (i. 5 ff.) to be His "Servant." He shrank from the hard task of this service, e.g. viii. 23 ff. (E.V. ix. 1 ff.).

> Óh that my héad were wáters,
> And mine éye a foúntain of téars,
> That by dáy and by níght I might wéep,
> For the sláin of the Daúghter of my Péople !
> Óh that I hád in the Wílderness
>   A wáyfarer's lódge !

That Í might forsáke my Péople,
    And gét me gone fróm them.
For théy are adúlterers áll,
    An assémbly of tráitors!

(xi. 19.)

Wóe is mé for my húrt! griévous my woúnd!
And I sáid, This is síckness, indéed; I must beár it.

(xii. 1.)

Ríghteous art Thoú O Jáhve,
Yét would I pléad with Thée;
And would tálk with Thée of júdgements:
Why próspers the wáy of the wícked?
Why are tráitors áll of them háppy?

There were times when Jeremiah rebelled against his task (xv. 10, 17 f.; xx. 7 ff.). But the thought that he was God's Servant helped him through, till God's word became not a "fire" (xx. 9) but the "joy and rejoicing of his heart" (xv. 16). Like Dante (*Purg.* xxvii.) he passed through the fire and found Paradise beyond.

This personal experience Jeremiah transferred to the People that he loved.

As God had called *him* from all eternity (i. 5 ff.) in spite of unworthiness, so God has called *Israel*—(xxxi. 2, see context).

  With eternal love have I loved thee
  And therefore with mercy have drawn thee.

The Prophet well knew the difficulty of this :

(xiii. 23.)

Can Éthiop chánge his skín,
              Or léopard his spóts ?
Then yé shall be fítted for góod
              that are wónted to évil.

Compare also xvii. 9, xxx. 12. But the very
difficulty made him the more certain that God must
act. Thus the Prophet who knew most of sin and
of sorrow reached the highest point of Old Testament
Revelation in the certainty of the New Covenant.

(xxxi. 33.)

I do sét My Láw withín them,
And ón their heárts I will wríte it ;
And Í will be theírs as Gód,
While théy shall be Míne as Péople.

But as, in Jeremiah's case, sufferings were the
mode of *service* through which he found God, so also
it must be in the case of the Nation : and I would
call special attention to the fact that *Jeremiah is the
first to apply the title "Thy Servant" to Israel* (see
Driver, *L.O.T.* p. 246), and that he does so in these
Chapters which speak of the New Covenant. Thus :

(xxx. 10 f.)

"And thou, My Servant Jacob, fear not, saith Jahve ;
dread not, O Israel, for it is I that am saving thee

from afar....Though I make a full end of all the Nations whither I have scattered thee, yet with thee I will not make a full end."

So, then, while Jeremiah gives no formal answer to the question, Why do the People of God suffer? his own experience suggests a very practical answer: Suffering is Service—Israel is (like the Prophet) God's *Servant*.

Of a life beyond the grave the Prophets had no certain knowledge. The Captivity was the *death* of Israel and it was a mighty venture of faith to believe that the "dead bones" could once more live (Ezek. xxxvii. 1—14).

Before considering the problem of suffering in the Book of Job we will give a translation of Ps. xxxix. which, more than any other Psalm, is full of the language and thought of Job. [See *Psalms in Three Collections*, pp. 155—160.]

I have followed Wellhausen in omitting *v.* 10 which seems to have been a gloss on *v.* 3. I have also placed the Refrain at the end of *v.* 7 instead of *v.* 6, where it interrupts the sense.

The division of the Psalm into three strophes is suggested by *v.* 13 "*My prayer*," "*My cry*," "*My tears*," in inverted order.

(Ps. xxxix.)

(My *tears, v.* 13.)

2 I saíd, I must héed my wáys, | not to sín with my tóngue.
I must kéep my moúth with a brídle, | While the wícked is
still in my présence.

3 I was útterly dúmb, | not spéaking a wórd ; | and my grief
grew inténse.

4 With heárt hot withín me, | fire kíndled with thoúght; | so
I spáke with my tóngue.

(My *cry*, v. 13.)

5 Shéw me, O Jáhve, mine énd, | and my pórtion of dáys what
it ís: | I would knów how fléeting I ám.

6 Behóld as a spán | Thou hast máde my dáys; | and my lífetime
is nóthing befóre Thee !

7 Man wálks in mere shów; | They are vaínly in túrmoil; | He
píles and he knóws not who gáthers !

A MERE BRÉATH IS MAN'S LÓT.

(My *prayer*, v. 13.)

8 And nów, Lord, whý do I wáit ? | —My hópe is in Thée!

9 Frée me from áll my transgréssions; | Make me nót a repróach
for the fóol.

11 Remóve from óff me Thy stróke; | 'Neath the weíght (?) of
Thine hánd I consúme.

12 With requítal of sín | Thou puníshest mán, | Dost wáste his
delíghts like the móth.

A MERE BRÉATH IS MAN'S LÓT.

13 Héar my práyer, O Jáhve ;
Give éar to my crý;
Bé not sílent to my téars ;

For Í am a guést with Thée,
Like áll my fáthers a sójourner.
14 Léave me spáce to take cómfort; | Befóre I depárt and I ám
      not!

We now turn to the Book of Job. The problem
that the writer had to solve was exactly that of the
Prophet Habakkuk—Why should Israel, righteous
by comparison, be of all Nations *the Suffering
Nation*?

To solve the problem he introduces a man "perfect
and upright" (i. 1) amongst men. In Heaven God
bears witness to him (i. 8) and the Accuser is allowed
to put him to the utmost test (i. 12, ii. 6). Then,
when every conceivable trouble and affliction has
fallen upon Job, his three friends who represent the
"wisdom" literature of the day come to comfort him.
This "wisdom" had, as we have seen, its origin in
the eudaemonism of Deuteronomy, of the Alphabetical
Psalms, of the Book of Proverbs, and other similar
works. The writer intends to allow this "Wisdom"
to speak for itself, and to find what it is worth by
applying it to the sufferings of a righteous man.
Job's three friends no doubt represent different
phases of this "wisdom," but for our present purpose
it will suffice to consider them as one.

The Poem begins at chapter III.

The friends at first insinuate, and afterwards
openly declare, that Job's sufferings must be due to
some great and flagrant sin.

Remémber; who éver hath pérished being ínnocent ?
Or whén were ríghteous men cut óff[1] ?

Compare also v. 2 with Ps. xxxvii. 1, 2, 7.

Temporal prosperity *must* be the portion of the
good (v. 19—27), otherwise where is God's justice ?

It is true that a wicked man (like Job) may seem
to prosper for a time, but this only means a sudden
and terrible fate that is coming upon him and on his
children (v. 3 ff.). Add to this the terrors of an evil
conscience (xv. 20 ff., xviii. 5—21).

All this is worked out with great power and
doubtless it represented the orthodox teaching of the
day. But Job will have none of it. Such arguments
are mere words (vi. 26, xvi. 3). He had hoped for
comfort from his friends but they have proved utterly
false ; vi. 15—20.

> My bróthers are decéitful as a tórrent;
> Like the chánnel of the bróoks they chánge:
> Which run dárk becaúse of the íce,
> And the snów that hídes itself ín them.
> They no sóoner are wárm than they vánish;
> When hót they are driéd from their pláce.
> The páths of their wáy are divérted ;
> They ascénd and pérish in vóid.
> The caraváns of Téman looked fór them ;
> The cómpanies of Shéba expécted them—
> They were shámed becaúse of their trúst;
> They cáme there and blúshed for sháme.

[1] Job iv. 7; cf. Ps. xxxvii. 25.

While freely admitting the general fact of sinfulness (ix. 2, xiii. 26), Job absolutely refused to admit the contention of his friends that his sufferings were the result of some grievous hidden sin.   He calls God to witness that it is not so.

(ix. 32 f.)

Were He óne like mysélf I would ánswer Him,
We would cóme togéther in júdgement.
But there ís betwíxt us no úmpire,
That can láy his hánd on us bóth.

(xiii. 15.)

Lo, He may sláy me, I cánnot hópe ;
Yet my wáys I maintáin to His Fáce.
He Himsélf should be míne for salvátion ;
For no hýpocrite cómes in His Présence.

Rather than admit what he knows to be untrue he would charge God with injustice.

(xix. 6.)

Knów then that Gód has wrónged me.

(xxvii. 3 ff.)

As lóng as my spírit is ín me,
And the bréath of Gód in my nóstrils,
My líps shall nót speak untrúth,
And my tóngue shall nót utter fálsehood,
Far bé it from mé to pronoúnce you ríght ;
Till I díe I will néver rejéct mine intégrity.

Job's apparent claim to sinlessness is exactly that of Israel in Pss. xvii. 1—5, xviii. 20 ff., xxvi., xliv. 17 ff., lxix. 7 ff., ci. In other words it is that of the "Servant" of God.

As to the assertion of the "friends" that prosperity is the lot of the righteous, Job positively asserts the very opposite. Thus:

(xxi. 7.)

7   Whý do the wícked have lífe?
     They grow óld, wax míghty in stréngth.
8   Their séed is estáblished before them;
     And their óffspring whíle they yet líve.
9   Their hoúses are sáfe from féar;
     And nó rod of Gód is on thém.

. . . .

12 They táke up the tábret and hárp;
     And rejoíce at the soúnd of the lúte.

. . ..

17 How óft is the lámp of the wícked extínguished?
     (Is it trué) that their fáte comes upón them?
     The pángs He distríbutes in ánger?

To Job the world is full of sadness: the bitter cry of the workers (chapter XXIV) reminds us of the *Song of the Shirt.*

12 From oút of the cíty men groán,
     And the sóul of the sláin crieth oút;
     Yet Gód impúteth no wróng!

The pathos of it all was intensified by the fact that to Job the grave was utterly dark.

(xiv. 7 ff.)

7 For the trée there máy be hópe;
  Though félled it agáin may sproút;
  And its ténder bránch not fáil.
8 Though its róot grow old in the éarth,
  And its stóck may díe in the groúnd.
9 Yet through scént of the wáter it búds,
  And púts forth its boúghs as when yoúng.
10 But a héro must díe and be wásted!
  Man gíves up the ghóst, and where ís he?
11 Wáters will have vánished from the séa;
  The Ríver will have wásted and be dríed;
12 But mán lies thére and ríseth not;
  While héaven exísts they wáke not,
  Nor cán they be roúsed from their sléep.

See also *vv.* 16—21.

Yet, in spite of the sufferings of the present, the falseness of his friends, and the darkness of the future, Job was sure of God; and because of this, his words gain meanings far beyond his thought.

(xvi. 19 ff.)

In the Héaven, even nów, is my Wítness,
In hígh-heaven my Téstimony.
With móckers for friénds!
Unto Gód doth mine éye drop téars,
For a Pléader for mán with Gód,
  A mán for his féllow!

Thus, in spite of some hasty words, Job, like Jeremiah, is faithful to the end; and poetic justice

requires that light should break. The light comes
through a Divine Voice (chapter XXXVIII f.) which
appeals, not as arguments to the mind, but as light
to the whole being. (Compare the conclusion of
Tennyson's *Two Voices.*) Driver (*L.O.T.*) well says
of these chapters : "The first speech of Jehovah
transcends all other descriptions of the wonders of
creation or the greatness of the Creator, which are
to be found either in the Bible or elsewhere. Parts
of 2 Isaiah (e.g. *c.* 40) approach it ; but they are
conceived in a different strain, and, noble as they
are, are less grand and impressive. The picturesque
illustrations, the choice diction, the splendid imagery,
the light and rapid movement of the verse, combine
to produce a whole of incomparable brilliancy and
force."

Before offering a translation of portions of this
speech I must ask the reader to remember that the
object of the Divine Voice is *not* to impress Job with
the *omnipotence* of God : for he well knew this, and
nothing could go beyond the power and beauty with
which he has already pictured the Divine omnipotence
in chapter XXXVI ending with the words

> Lo thése are but párts of His wáys ;
> The mere whísper aboút Him that's héard :
> But the thúnder of His míght, who can knów ?

If the Divine Voice had taught nothing more than
omnipotence it would have been no *revelation*. But

it suggests throughout, *a Divine purpose and care lying behind the power.* And this is just what the sufferer needs to rebuke his faithless fears.

(Job xxxviii. 2 ff.)

God's Voice out of the Storm.

2   Who ís it that dárkeneth coúnsel
      With wórds without knówledge ?
3   Gírd now thy loíns like a mán:
      I will ásk : do thou ánswer.

Earth implies a purpose.

4   Where wért thou when éarth was foúnded ?
      Decláre if thou skillést to knów.
5   Who appoínted the méasures she ówns ?
      Or whó stretched the líne upón her ?
6   Her foundátions, on whát were they séttled ?
      Or whó laid her córner stóne ?
7   While the mórning-stars sáng in chórus
      And the sóns-of-God shoúted for jóy !

The Sea proclaims the Creator's purpose in curbing it.

8   When He shút up with dóors the Séa
      That búrst, as it wére, from a wómb ?
9   When I máde the cloúd its vésture ;
      And dárkness its swáddling-bánd ?
10   When I clénched on it Mý decrée,
      And appoínted it bárs and dóors ?
      [and said]
11   Thus fár shalt thou cóme and no fúrther ;
      And hére shall thy proúd waves be stáyed ?

The creation of light implies the victory of all good.

12   Couldst thoú ever give chárge to the Mórning;
     Or téach the Dáwn its pláce?

13   How to grásp the córners of éarth
     Till the wícked be sháken thereoút?

14   It is chánged like the cláy of a seál;
     Things stand oút as though clóthed with a gárment!

15   While their líght is withhéld from the wícked,
     And the árm that is lófty is bróken.

The Under-world, a storehouse for good ends.

16   Hast thou éntered the mázes of Séa?
     Or wálked the recésses of the Déep?

17   Have the gátes of Déath been reveáled to thee?
     Canst thou sée the gátes of Death-shádow?

18   Canst thoú comprehénd to earth's boúnds?
     Téll then if thou knówest her whólly.

19   Whére is the wáy where light dwélleth?
     And dárkness, whére is its pláce?

20   That thoú shouldst condúct it to boúnds
     And shouldst knów the páths to its dwélling!

21   Dost thou knów it as béing then bórn?
     Is the númber of thy dáys so mány?

22   Hast thou éntered the stórehouse of snów?
     And the stórehouse of háil, hast thou séen it?

23   Which for tíme of stréss I am kéeping,
     For the dáy of báttle and wár.

24   Whích is the wáy light is párted,
     When it scátters the stórmblast on earth?

25   Who ópened the chánnel of cloúdburst,
     And the wáy for the flásh of the thúnder?

26   Causing ráin on lánd without mán,
     On úninhábited wílderness!

27   Sóaking the désolate wáste
     Till it spríng with gérms of gráss!
28   Háth the ráin a fáther?
     Or whó hath begótten the déw-drops?
29   The íce? from whose wómb came it fórth?
     The hóar-frost of héaven? who géndered it?
30   The wáters are hídden like stóne
     And the fáce of the déep is congéaled.

The Upper-world also declares the purpose of its Maker.

31   Canst thou fásten the bánds of the Pleíades?
     Or lóosen the fétters of Oríon?
32   Canst bring éach constellátion in séason?
     Canst guíde Arctúrus with his sóns?
33   Dost thou knów the státutes of héaven?
     Canst thou fíx each ínfluence over éarth?
34   Canst thou líft up thy voíce to the cloúds,
     That abúndance of wáter may cóver thee?
35   The líghtnings? canst sénd that they gó?
     That they ánswer thee, Hére we áre?
36   Who gáve them their ínward wísdom?
     Or impárted a mínd-like intélligence?

The poem passes on to depict God's care manifested in the instinct He has implanted in the lion,
the raven, the hinds, and other creatures of the
wilderness, and closes with a magnificent passage
which we must translate:

(xxxix. 19 ff.)

19   Couldst thou gíve to the hórse his stréngth?
     Couldst thou clóthe his néck as with thúnder?

Couldst thou gíve him the rústle of lócusts ?
That glóry and térror of nóstril !
He páweth in the válley and exúlteth in his stréngth,
He rúsheth to fáce the wéapons.
He mócketh at féar and is not dismáyed,
Nor túrneth he báck from the swórd.
Agáinst him the quíver may ríng,
The fláme of the spéar and the jávelin :
With fúrious ónset he devoúrs the gróund,
For he cánnot be stíll when the trúmpet soúnds.
In the thíck of the trúmpets he saith, Ahá !
For he scénteth the báttle from afár,
The thúnder of cáptains and shoút of wár.

Thus, as far as the Book of Job is concerned, the answer to the problem of suffering is given not to the intellect but to the eye of faith. Job might have said with Browning's *Rabbi ben Ezra* :

" I, who saw power, see now love perfect too :
　　Perfect I call Thy plan :
　　Thanks that I was a man !
Maker, remake, complete,—I trust what Thou shalt do ! "

Next in order of thought, and probably in order of time, comes the Evangelical Prophet, generally known as the Second Isaiah who prophesied during the closing years of the Captivity (*c.* 538 B.C.) and completed the mission of Jeremiah.

We have already seen (p. 78) that Jeremiah was the first to speak of Israel as God's "Servant" who should suffer but should not be destroyed. But

Jeremiah attributes no *atoning value* to those
sufferings. He pictures more fully than any other
the "glories that shall follow," but he leaves the
mind unsatisfied as to the justice of the suffering.
Not so the Evangelical Prophet whose position in the
Old Testament is unique.

The key-note of the Evangelical Prophet is struck
in the opening words of his Prophecy in which,
measuring Jerusalem's guilt with the guilt of the
Nations, he boldly declares that her sufferings have
more than atoned for it, and that those sufferings are
being used by God for the furtherance of His Glory
in the world (cf. Col. i. 24).

(Is. xl. 1.)

Cómfort ye, cómfort ye My Péople,
          Saíth your Gód.
Spéak to the heárt of Jerúsalem,
          And procláim unto hér
That her sérvice is accómplished | That her guílt is atóned,
That she tóok at Jáhve's hánd,
          The doúble of her síns.

He sees Israel as the "Servant" with a mission
to the Gentiles ; a Servant blind to the Master's
purpose, yet privileged to bring through his own
sufferings, the knowledge of God to all the Nations
of the earth. The following passages may suffice to
make this clear.

(Is. xli. 8 f.)

And Ísrael, thoú art My Sérvant;
The Jácob whóm I have chósen;
The séed of Ábraham My friénd;
Thoú that I fétched from far lánds,
And cálled from the cónfines thereóf,
And saíd to thee, Thoú art My Sérvant,
I chóse thee and háve not rejécted thee.

In Abraham "all the families of the earth" are
to be blessed. Abraham's "seed" is "elect" to carry
out this purpose.

(Is. xlii. 1 ff.)

1   Lo! My Sérvant whom Í uphóld,
    The Eléct My Sóul is well pléased in;
    I have pút My Spírit upón him,
    He will bríng forth ríght to the Géntiles.

2   He sháll not crý nor clámour,
    Nor make héard his voíce in the stréet;

3   He dóes not breák a crushed réed,
    Nor quénch a glímmering wíck;
    But in trúth he bríngs forth ríght.

4   He will nót be dím or crúshed
    Till he stáblish the ríght upon éarth,
    And the coúntries awáit his téaching.
         .   .   .   .

6   I Jáhve have cálled thee in ríghteousness,
    Have hólden thy hánd and will kéep thee,
    And will máke thee a cóvenant-péople,
                 a líght for the Géntiles;

7   To ópen éyes that are blínd,
    To bríng forth the cáptive from príson,
    And from dúngeon those sítting in dárkness.

In xliii. 10 the singular and plural are applied to
Israel, "Ye are My witnesses, saith Jahve, and (ye
are) My Servant whom I have chosen."

The success of the Servant's missionary work is
pictured as follows:

(Is. xliv. 1 ff.)

1   But héar now, O Jácob My Sérvant;
     And Ísrael whóm I have chósen.
2   Thús saith Jáhve thy Máker,
     He that fórmed thee from bírth and will hélp thee;
     Féar not, thou Jácob My Sérvant,
     Jeshúrun whóm I have chósen;
3   For wáter I póur on the thírsty,
     And stréams on the drý-land;
     I will póur on thy séed My Spírit,
     Ánd, on thy óffspring, My bléssing:
4   They shall shóot up as wátered gráss;
     As póplars by wáter-cóurses.
5   Thís one shall sáy, I am Jáhve's;
     Anóther shall célebrate Jácob;
     Anóther inscríbes himself Jáhve's,
     And takes Ísrael's náme as a súrname.

The missionary work of the Servant results in the
conversion of Egypt, Ethiopia and the Sabeans (xlv.
14) and indeed of all the Nations (xlii. 4, 10, 12).

(Is. xlix. 1 ff.)

1   Heárken ye lánds unto mé!
     Give éar ye péoples from afár!
     Jáhve called mé from the wómb;
     From my bírth He méntioned my náme:

2   And He máde my moúth a sharp swórd;
      In the sháde of His hánd He híd me,
      And He máde me a pólished árrow,
      In His quíver concéaled me, and saíd,
3   O Ísrael thoú art My sérvant
      Through whóm I máke Myself glórious.
4   [Whereas I thought]
      I have láboured in váin in vóid,
      Have spént my stréngth for nóthing;
      And yét my ríght was with Jáhve,
      My rewárd was wíth my Gód.
5   And now thus saith Jáhve—
      That fórmed me from bírth as His Sérvant
      To bríng back Jácob to Hím,
      And the Ísrael nót yet gáthered:
      And só I am hónoured in Jáhve's eyes,
      And my Gód is becóme my stréngth.
6   And He said,
      'Tis éasy, for thée to be Sérvant,
      To ráise up the tríbes of Jácob,
      And to restóre the rémnant of Ísrael,
      But I máke thee a líght of the Géntiles,
      To becóme My salvátion to the énds of the éarth.

These last verses involve a certain difficulty; for if the Servant be the ideal Israel, how can he be said to bring back Israel? To this I would reply that the Ten Tribes had been practically lost in the Captivity and that the Prophets naturally expected a reunion so that "all Israel should be saved." This was to be brought about by the Servant. But the hard portion of his task was to be the conversion of the Gentiles.

This would involve him in suffering. So the passage continues:

> 7 Thus saith Jahve :—
> Ísrael's Góêl and Hóly One—
> Of one despísed and abhórred of péople,
>   of a sérvant of déspots—
> Kíngs shall sée and rise úp,
>   and prínces pay réverence.

In other words the Servant who had been oppressed and despised by the kings of the earth will be seen by them at last, and confessed with wonder as the world's redeemer.

The Servant had been "blind" to this good purpose of God.

(Is. xlii. 19.)

> Whó is so blínd as My Sérvant?

But when led to see, he will accept his mission as a Sufferer, and the sacrifice will become joy.

(Is. l. 5 f.)

> Jáhve hath ópened mine éar—
> I díd not rebél, nor túrn awáy báck:
> I gáve my báck to the smíters, | My chéeks to the péeling;
> I híd not my fáce from spítting and sháme.

We are now in a position to consider the famous passage Is. lii. 13—liii.

This poem is complete in itself. It may be removed from its context without disturbing the sense

Indeed some scholars have regarded it as a quotation. But this is, I think, a mistake; for as I have tried to shew, the whole argument has been leading up to it.

(Is. lii. 13 ff.)

STROPHE I. *God is pictured as speaking.*

13   Behóld My Sérvant shall prósper;
      Shall be hígh and uplífted, excéedingly lófty.
14   As dumbfoúnded at thée were the MÁNY—
      So márred more than húman his vísage,
      And his fórm more than sóns of mén—
15   So (nów) he astoúnds MANY nátions;
      At hím kings wónder in sílence:
      [lit. "shut their mouth at him"]
      For a thíng untóld do they sée;
      An unhéard of thíng do they pónder.

STROPHE II.   *The many Nations of the world as represented*
              by their kings now speak.

Ch. liii.

1   Whó could have belíeved this good-néws of ours?
     And Jáhve's arm, on whóm hath it been revéaled?
2   He (i.e. Israel) came úp before Hím as a plánt;
     As a róot from groúnd that is drý.
     No fórm or spléndour was hís | that wé
                              should regárd him!
     Nor áspect, that wé should desíre him!
3   Despísed and desérted by mén!
     A mán of sórrows, and wónted to síckness!
     As óne from whom (Gód's) Face was hídden!
     Despísed, and we coúnted him nót!

STROPHE III. *The Nations now see that Israel, whom they despised, has been, all along, the scape-goat for the world.*

4   But oúr síckness[1] HÉ hath bórne !
     And oúr sórrows[1] HÉ hath cárried !
     While wÉ regárded him as léprous;
     Strícken of Gód and afflícted !
5   While HÉ was piérced by our síns;
     Brúised by oúr iníquities !
     The chástisement of our péace was on hím;
     And his strípes were héaling for ús.
6   All wé had wándered like shéep ;
     Éach his own wáy we had túrned;
     And Jáhve caúsed to méet on hím the sín
                         of áll of ús.

STROPHE IV. *The Nations ponder with wonder over the meekness and gentleness of the Sufferer. (Verses 8 ab, 9 ab are difficult and possibly corrupt. I leave them unaccented.)*

7   When oppréssed he ónly húmbled himsélf,
     And woúld not ópen his moúth.
     As a shéep that is broúght to the slaúghter,
     As a éwe that is dúmb to her shéarers,
     So he woúld not ópen his moúth.
8   Without rúle without ríght was he táken
     And his generation who could declare ?
     For he was cút from the lánd of the líving,
     For the sín of the péoples, the plágue that was théirs.
9   So the wicked were given for his grave (?)
     And the rich for his (many) deaths[2]
     Becaúse that no víolence[3] he díd, nor was fraúd in his
                         moúth.

[1] See *v.* 3.   [2] Ezek. xxviii. 10.   [3] Job xvi. 17.

K.   7

STROPHE V. *Here, as in strophe I the point of view is not that of the Nations of the world but of God Himself who becomes the actual speaker in vv.* 11, 12.

10 And Jáhve wílled to brúise[1] him;
        Hé caused the síckness[2]:
    Íf his sóul would máke itself an óffering
    A séed he should behóld should háve long lífe
    And the wíll of Jáhve by hís means should prósper:

11 Of the trávail of his sóul he should sée and be contént,
    By his (?its) knówledge should My Sérvant máke the
        MANY[3] ríghteous;
    And théir iniquíties he himsélf shall cárry[4].

12 Thérefore I allót him his pórtion with the MANY[5],
    Ánd with the míghty hé divides the spoíl;
    Becaúse that hé hath émptied his sóul unto the déath,
    And was númbered with transgréssors.
    So hé himsélf the sín of MANY[5] báre
    And só atónes transgréssors.

The reader will notice that the word "Many" occurs five times in this Poem, twice in strophe I and three times in strophe V. In strophe I "the many" were the Nations of the World whose look of pitying contempt shall be changed to a look of adoring wonder. In strophe V we learn how this has come about. The "Servant" has cast in his portion with "the many." He has borne the sin of "the many," and so has made "the many" acceptable

[1] *v.* 5.   [2] *v.* 3 f.   [3] *vv.* 14, 15.
[4] *v.* 4.   [5] *v.* 11.

to God. Thus by the obedience of the One the Many
are made righteous (cf. Rom. v. 15).

There is nothing in the history of prophecy more
remarkable than the small effect produced by these
wonderful Chapters of the Suffering Servant. No
doubt we may in part account for this by the fact
that Persia the deliverer soon became Persia the
persecutor, and the sense of Israel's mission to the
Gentiles was lost in bitterness. But for the true
cause we must look deeper and regard it as a
"mystery" hidden in God to await the fulness of
Christian times. Meanwhile the prophecy is there.
It is

"...music sent up to God by the lover and the bard;
Enough that He heard it once; we shall hear it by and by."

The suffering of the good, and the prosperity of
evil-doers, tended at a later time to direct the thoughts
of men to the life beyond the grave. We will give
one illustration of this from the Asaph Psalms which
I would assign to *c.* 450 B.C. The Psalm (lxxiii.) is
interesting not only for its subject-matter but also
for its metre.

(Ps. lxxiii.)

1   Mere góodness is Gód unto Ísrael,
                To the Púre in heárt!
2   As for mé—my féet had nigh góne;
      My stéps had áll but slípped.

3 For I énvied the lót of the proúd;
   The péace of the wícked I sáw.
4 For pángs are nót for thém;
   Soúnd and robúst is their héalth.
5 No sháre have théy in man's toíl,
   Nor áre they strícken like óthers.
6 Thérefore doth príde bedéck them;
   Víolence enróbes them as a gárment.
7 Their iníquity proúdly goes fórth:
   They excéed all heárt can pícture.
8 They móck while they wíckedly spéak;
   They lóftily spéak their oppréssion.
9 They have sét their moúth against héaven;
   And their tóngue goes the círcuit of éarth.
10 Therefore... [*text doubtful*]
   .   .   .   .
11 And they sáy, "How thén can God knów?
               Has Elyón percéption?"

12 Behóld the wícked are thús!
   Éver at péace they grow stróng!
13 Then váinly I cléanse my heárt,
   And wásh my hánds in ínnocency;
14 While Í am strícken all dáy,
   My chástisement mórn by mórn!

15 Trúly were Í to speak thús
   I were fálse to the generátion of Thy chíldren.
16 Yet, whén I bethoúght me to knów this,
   Griévous it wás in mine éyes;
17 Till I cáme to the Sánctuary of Gód—
               I thoúght on their énd!
18 Mérely 'mid delúsions Thou dost pláce them—
             Dost cást them to rúin!

19 How súdden they cóme to destrúction—
          Are énded with térror!
20 When roúsed Thou spúrnest their ímage
          Like a dréam on awáking!
21 Indéed, when my heárt was embíttered,
          And my reíns were pertúrbed,
22 Then Í—I was brútish and knéw not—
          I becáme as the béasts!
23 Yet Í—am éver with Thée;
          Thou uphóldest my hánd;
24 With Thy coúnsel dost guíde me; and áfter
          Wilt táke me in glóry.
25 Who is míne in the héavens?
      And, with Thée, I desíre naught on éarth.
26 My flésh and my heárt may consúme,
      Yet the Róck of my heárt and my pórtion
          Elŏhím is for éver!

27 For behóld! Thy divórced-ones must pérish;
      Thou destróyest each whóring from Thée.
28 But for mé—the néarness of Gód is my góod;
      In Jáhve, the Lórd, do I sét my réfuge.

The metre of this Psalm is irregular. It opens
with the *Ḳínah* measure, after which we have several
verses in triplets. Then *vv.* 17—24, a fine passage
of *Ḳínah*, after which we have further irregularity.
Whether this be due to corruption of the text or to
the intention of the writer we cannot now determine.
Our present object is to consider the Psalm merely in
regard to the problem of the sufferings of the righteous,
i.e. Israel.

Verse 1 states the eternal truth ; *vv.* 2—11 the apparent exception which creates the difficulty. In *vv.* 12—14 the Psalmist speaking for Israel, confesses the temptation to doubt the eternal truth of *v.* 1. If he were to yield to that temptation he feels that he would be a traitor to the cause of God (*v.* 15), and yet he, like Job, feels the difficulty most keenly (*v.* 16). The solution comes (*vv.* 17 ff.) when he enters into "the Sanctuary of God." By this we must not understand *the Temple* but rather the *Sanctuary- purpose* of God's creative thought. The Psalmist, like Dante, must " see the children of perdition" (*Purg.* xxx. end). The solution reached by the Psalmist differs from that of Job and indicates a later date. It is nothing less than this—The wicked have no reality of existence, they are but a dream of God (*v.* 20), which when He wakes He puts away[1], whereas Israel, the righteous, is an Enoch who "walks with God" (*v.* 24), and being "joined unto the Lord" is "one Spirit" with Him (*v.* 28, cf. 1 Cor. vi. 17). Thus the Psalm returns (*v.* 28) to the thought with which it commenced; God *is* "good to Israel" and Israel's "good" is the "nearness of God." If the Psalmist did not reach to the Christian conception of *personal* immortality, he had at least the root of the matter in Israel's union with God.

[1] Compare Shakespeare, *Second Part of King Henry IV*, Scene V, lines 50—54.

CHAPTER VI

ON THE STROPHE

It may be well, at once, to define the sense in which we apply the word *strophe* to Hebrew poetry since it differs somewhat from the clearly defined *strophe* and *antistrophe* of the classical writers.

The Hebrew *strophe* is a development of *parallelism*. That which parallelism is to the ear in the structure of the verse, that the *strophe* is to the mind in the arrangement of the whole poem. This balance of thought is sometimes marked by a *refrain* and is found not only in the lyric poetry of the Psalms but also in the rhetorical poetry of the Prophets[1]. Thus:

(Amos vii. 1—9, viii. 1—3.)

STROPHE I.

1 Thus hath the Lord God shewed me:
  And behold He was framing the locust at the early shooting of the latter-growth;
  And behold it was the latter-growth after the king's mowings.
2 So it was when it finished to eat all the grass of the land,
  Then I said, O Lord God, forgive now;
  How shall Jacob stand? for he is small!
3 (Then) *Jahve repented of this:*
  It shall not be, saith Jahve.

  [1] See Dr D. H. Müller, *Komposition und Strophenbau.*

STROPHE II.

4　Thus hath the Lord God shewed me:
　　And behold He was calling to contend by fire,
　　And it devoured the great deep
　　And was eating the land.
5　*Then I said, O Lord God, cease now;*
　　How shall Jacob stand? for he is small!
6　(Then) *Jahve repented of this :*
　　This too shall not be, saith Jahve.

Here we have two strophes of eight lines each,
closing with the same refrain. In the same way
vv. 7—9 form another strophe of eight lines corresponding with viii. 1—3, as follows:

STROPHE III.

7　Thus He (the Lord God) shewed me ;
　　And behold He stood on a plumbline wall, with a plumbline
　　　　in hand.
8　And Jahve said to me, What seest thou, Amos ?
　　And I answered, A plumbline.
　　And the Lord said, Lo I am setting a plumbline in the
　　　　midst of My people Israel ;
　　I will not again pass by them.
9　And Isaac's shrines shall be desolate, and the sanctuaries of
　　　　Israel waste ;
　　And I rise against the house of Jeroboam with the sword.

STROPHE IV (Chap. viii. 1—3).

1　Thus the Lord God shewed me ;
　　And behold a basket of *endings*[1].

---

[1] "*Endings*," lit. *summer-fruit*, so called because it comes at the
end of the year. I have coined the word *endings* in order to preserve
the play upon the word *end* which occurs in the Hebrew.

2 And He said, What seest thou, Amos?
  And I answered, A basket of *endings*.
  And Jahve said to me, The *end* is coming for My people
    Israel;
  I will not again pass by them.
3 And the Temple songs shall be howlings in that day, saith
    the Lord God.
  Many the corpses, in every place, one casts them forth with
    silence.

A fine example of the prophetical use of the refrain is found in Is. ix. 7—20. I have based my translation upon the critical edition of the Hebrew text in "The Sacred Books of the Old Testament." The rhetoric of the Prophet becomes lyric through intensity of feeling.

7 The Lórd sent a wórd into Jácob,
    And it líghted on Ísrael.
8 And the whóle of the Péople shall knów,
    Even Éphraim and the dwéllers in Samária
    That [stíffen their nécks] with príde
    Saying thús, in stoútness of heárt;—
9   Brícks have fáiled | hewn-stóne we buíld;
    Felléd are the sýcomores; | we repláce them with cédars.
10 So Jáhve sets úp his [énemies] agáinst him,
    And his fóes He incítes.
11 Édom in frónt | and the Phílistine behínd,
    And they éat up Ísrael, open-moúthed.
    For all thís His ánger turns nót,
    But His hánd is strétched out stíll.
12 Yet the Péople turns nót to its Smíter,
    And séeks not to Jáhve.

13 So He cúts from Ísrael héad and táil
   Pálm-branch and rúsh, in one dáy!

   .   .   .   .

16 For 'tis whólly víle and évil;
   And évery moúth speaketh fólly.
   For all thís His ánger turns nót,
   But His hánd is strétched out still.

17 For wíckedness búrneth like fíre
   That devoúreth bríer and thórn
   When it kíndles the thíckets of the fórest
   Till they moúnt in píllars of smóke.

18ᵃ Through Jáhve's wráth shall the Lánd be kíndled,
   And the péople be as fúel for the fíre,

19 When it snátches on the ríght, but húngers,
   And devoúreth on the léft, unsátisfied.

18ᶜ So nó man hath píty on bróther;
   Each devoúrs the flésh of his [féllow];

20 Manásseh, Éphraim; and Éphraim, Manásseh;
   And bóth against Júdah togéther!
   For all thís His ánger turns nót,
   But His hánd is strétched out still.

(Chap. x.)

1 Ho! you decreérs of unríghteous decrées!
   Indíters of édicts oppréssive!

2 Thrústing the féeble from jústice,
   And stéaling the ríght of My póor!
   So that wídows becóme their spoíl,
   And the fátherless théy may rób!

3 Whát will ye dó in the dáy of visitátion,
   The desolátion that cómes from afár?
   To whóm will ye flée as a réfuge?
   And whére will ye léave your wéalth?

4 . . . .
> *For all this His ánger turns nót,*
> *But His hánd is strétched out stíll.*

Even in the Book of Proverbs we find instances
of strophical arrangement. The Wisdom literature,
regarded as poetry, is somewhat stiff and pedantic, as
we have already seen in the Alphabetical Psalms, but
it represents a phase of Judaism, influenced probably in its later form by Greek thought, which is well
worthy of study. I select as an example the famous
Wisdom-passage in Prov. viii. The word which we
translate *"workman"* (E.V. *"one brought up"*), in
v. 30, is not altogether certain, but, in other passages,
we find the thought of Wisdom as a *builder* and as
cooperating with God in Creation. Thus:

(Prov. xxiv. 3.)

> Through Wísdom is buílded the hoúse,
> And stáblished it ís by discrétion.

Compare Jer. x. 12, li. 15 where almost the same
words are applied to God as the Creator of the World.

Also (Prov. iii. 19.)

> Jáhve through Wísdom built éarth;
> Through discrétion He stáblished the héavens.

And (Prov. ix. 1.)

> Wísdom hath buílded her hoúse;
> Hath héwn out her séven píllars.

We now offer a translation of Prov. viii. 1 ff.

(Prov. viii. Metre 3 + 3.)

STROPHE I. *In praise of Wisdom.*

1 Dóth not Wísdom crý, | and Prúdence útter her voíce?
2 In the chiéf of the públic high-pláces, | she stándeth amíd
   the páths;
3 By the Cíty éntrance gátes, | at the ópening of the dóors she
   cries;—
4 Unto yoú, O mén, I cáll; | and my voíce is to sóns of mén.
5 O ye símple, give héed unto prúdence, | and, ye fóols, prepáre
   your heárts.
6 Héar, for I spéak a vérity (?) | and the ópening of my líps is
   équity.
7 For 'tis trúth that my moúth shall útter, | while wíckedness
   is abhórred by my líps.
8 All the wórds of my moúth are in ríghtness, | naúght in
   them cróoked or fróward.
9 They are áll of them pláin to the wíse, | and ríght to thém
   that find knówledge.
10 Accépt ye my téaching—not sílver— | and knówledge pre-
    férred to choice-góld[1].

STROPHE II. *Wisdom in relation to man.*

12 Í [Wisdom] do neíghbour with Prúdence, | knówledge and
    discrétion I attáin.
13 Arrógance, príde, and wrong-dóing, | and the fróward moúth,
    do I háte.
14 Coúnsel is míne, and sound-knówledge, | míne (is) under-
    stánding and míght.
15 Through mé kíngs do reígn, | and prínces ríghtly bear swáy.
16 Through mé rúlers do rúle, | and nóbles góvern jústly.

---

[1] I agree with Müller in rejecting *v.* 11 as a gloss introduced from
chapter iii. 14 f.

17 Í love thém that love mé, | and my díligent-séekers shall
     fínd me.
18 Wéalth and hónour are míne, | dúrable ríches and ríghteous-
     ness.
19 My frúit is bétter than fínest-gold, | my próduce than choícest
     sílver.
20 In the wáy that is ríght I gó, | in the mídst of the páths of
     júdgement :
21 To gíve the trúe-wealth to my friénds, | and to fíll their
     tréasuries fúll.

STROPHE III. *Wisdom in relation to God.*

22 Jáhve gat Mé at the fírst, | befóre His wórks of yóre.
23 From of óld was I móulded— | from the fírst begínnings of
     éarth :
24 While as yét were no déeps was I fórmed, | when no foúntains
     aboúnded (?) with wáter :
25 E'er the moúntains' foundátions were láid, | befóre the hílls
     was I frámed :
26 Befóre He made éarth and fiélds, | and the tópmost dúst of
     the wórld.
27 There was Í when He frámed the héavens, | when He círcled
     the fáce of the déep :
28 When He sét the sky fírm up abóve, | when He stréngthened
     the wélls of the déep¹ :
29 When He máde for the Séa His láw, | that its wáters should
     nót excéed : | when he láwed the foundátions of éarth.
30 Then was Í, His wórkman, bý Him, | rejoícing befóre Him at
     áll times :
31 Rejoícing in the wórld of His éarth, | my delíghts being the
     sóns of mén.

¹ *v.* 28ᵇ. This reads like a gloss to explain *v.* 27ᵇ. The superfluous member of *v.* 29, i.e. *v.* 29ᶜ would read better here.

Here we have three clearly marked strophes of *ten lines* each. The first strophe may be regarded as introductory in praise of wisdom. The second strophe treats of wisdom on earth, in relation to man, while the third strophe treats of wisdom in Heaven, in relation to God. Compare the Alphabetical Psalms cxi. and cxii. I have shewn in my Introduction to the Alphabetical Psalms that the number *ten*, the number of the Covenant, plays a most important part in their arrangement (see *Psalms in Three Collections*, pp. 26—49). The writer of Prov. viii. belonged to the same school and would be influenced by similar motives.

The next illustration we shall take will be Psalm xlvi. in which the original metre is clearly

$$(2+2)+(2+2)$$

with a ring that reminds us of the Anapaest.

This Psalm, however, contains some lines in the more common metre of $3+3$ which seem to interrupt the sense, and which may possibly be due to a later writer. Since our present object is to illustrate the metre I shall, in my translation, avail myself of Rothstein's Hebrew Text and shall omit the portions which he marks in smaller type as not belonging to the original Poem, while I refer the Hebrew scholar to his critical notes. Rothstein regards the refrain as $3+3$ metre. Thus:

Jáhve of Hósts is wíth us | our Tówer is Jácob's Gód.

I would, however, call attention to the fact that the Divine Names, which may have been written with abbreviations, are peculiarly uncertain.

(Ps. xlvi.)

Metre (2+2)+(2+2). Refrain 3+3.

2 Jáhve is oúrs, | a réfuge and a stréngth, |
    a hélp in distrésses | most réady to be foúnd.
Thérefore we féar not, | though éarth suffer chánge, |
    though moúntains remóve | to the heárt of the séas.
[Jáhve of Hósts is wíth us, | our tówer is Jácob's Gód.]

4 Wáters may ráge, | moúntains may quáke |
    at the swélling of the Ríver, | the ráging of its wáves.
7 Nátions may ráge, | kíngdoms be móved | —
    He úttérs His voíce | éarth is dissólved!
8 Jáhve of Hósts is wíth us | our tówer is Jácob's Gód.

9 Cóme ye and sée | the dóings of Jáhve, |
    who quíeteth wár | to remótest éarth.
11 Be stíll and knów | that Í am Gód ; |
    exálted 'mid the Nátions, | exálted in the éarth.
12 Jáhve of Hósts is wíth us, | our tówer is Jácob's Gód.

I do not pledge myself to accept all Rothstein's emendations but they are certainly of interest as shewing the value of metrical study in textual criticism.

If we admit that the Psalm has been revised I would suggest that the object of the revision was to connect it with such passages as Is. xxxiii. 20 ff. where

God Himself is the "River" that lends such security
to Jerusalem. Thus :

> 20 Thine éyes shall sée Jerúsalem
> A quíet abóde, a tént that remóveth not,
> Whose pégs are néver drawn oút,
> And nóne of whose córds become rént.
>
> 21 For thére (as) a Ríver Jáhve is oúrs,
> A pláce of canáls, wíde-réaching ;
> Whereín no tríreme can cóme
> Nor can wár-ship pass throúgh it.
>
> 22 For Jáhve our júdge—
> Jáhve our léader—
> Jáhve our Kíng—
> Hé (it is) will sáve us.

This passage is not without difficulty (see Hebrew
text in *Sacred Books of O. T.*) but the general sense
is clear.   Other cities, like Babylon, Thebes, or Tyre,
were protected by mighty waters ; Jerusalem had no
River, but, better far, had the protection of God.

Other instances of the use of a refrain will be
found in Pss. xxxix. 6, 12 (5, 11); xlii. 6, 12 (5, 11),
with xliii. 5; xlix. 13, 21 (12, 20); lvi. 5, 11 (4, 11);
lvii. 6, 12 (5, 11); lix. 7, 15 (6, 14); 10, 18 (9, 17);
lxii. 3, 7 (2, 6); lxvii. 4, 6 (3, 5); lxxx. 4, 8, 20 (3, 7,
19); lxxxvii. 4^c, 6^c; xcix. 3^c, 5^c, 9^c; cvii. 6, 13, 19, 28
and 8, 15, 21, 31; cxvi. 13^b f., 17^b f. Also the response
throughout Ps. cxxxvi.

Some of these passages are treated at length in
other chapters (see pp. 50 ff.; 80 ; 114 f.) and, indeed,

the whole of our chapter on Alphabetical Poetry is
an illustration of the Hebrew strophe.

Ps. xcix. is specially interesting as an example of
the strophe marked by a refrain. In the present text
the refrain occurs three times and in an augmented
form. Thus the Psalm is divided into three strophes,
the first two being nearly equal, while the third is a
double strophe. Many commentators (Wellhausen,
Duhm, &c.) assume that what I have called a double
strophe was originally divided by a refrain, which has
been lost, after *v.* 7. But this, I think, is a mistake.
The thrice-repeated "Holy" (*vv.* 3, 5, 9) is, as in Is.
vi., the cry of the Cherubim who are mentioned in
v. 1. As, in Is. vi., the Angels acclaim the Advent of
God's "Glory" on earth, so, in the present Psalm, the
trisagion acclaims His coming Kingdom.

In strophe I the thought centres upon the *power*
of the Divine King; in strophe II upon His *justice*;
in strophe III upon His *mercy*. Thus the trisagion
of the refrain acclaims three aspects of the Divine
Nature.

The opening words of *v.* 1 denote, in the original,
not the mere fact of Jahve's Kingship, but rather,
that *His reign on earth has begun.* The Psalm
belongs to a group of Psalms which we might call the
Psalms of the Kingdom of God.

A question arises as to the metre of the Psalm.
Undoubtedly the greater part is in beats of *two*

K.   8

accents, but, in *vv.* 5, 6 and 9, we have lines of *three* accents. Is this due to a revision of the Psalm or was it the intention of the original writer?

Verse 6 might be literally translated

> "Moses and Aaron *among* His priests
> And Samuel *among* the Callers on His Name,"

but the Hebrew idiom rather signifies that Moses and Aaron were *chiefest* of His priests and that Samuel was *chiefest* of those that intercede. Thus they represent types of intercession.

(Ps. xcix.   Metre $(2+2)+(2+2)$ with occasional passages of $3+3$.)

STROPHE I.   *The holiness of God in His power.*

1   Jáhve is Kíng, | though the Péoples may ráge; | He is thróned on the Chérub, | though éarth may be móved.

2   Jáhve in Zíon | is greát and exálted ; | exálted is Hé | abóve all the Péoples.

3   They práise Thy Náme, | the greát and the térrible : | HÓLY IS HÉ.

STROPHE II.   *The holiness of God in His justice.*

4   [Thoú art] the Kíng | that lóvest ríght.—
    Thoú hast estáblished | équity (and) jústice ; | ríghteousness in Jácob | Thoú hast wroúght.

5   *Exált ye Jáhve our Gód*
    And bów at the stóol of His féet
        HÓLY IS HÉ.

STROPHE III. *The holiness of God in His mercy.*

6 Móses and Aáron His priésts;
And Sámuel amóng intercéssors;
To Jáhve they crý | and Hé gives them ánswer;
7 In the píllar of cloúd | He spéaks with thém:
They képt His téstimonies | and a státute He gáve them.
8 Jáhve, our Gód, | Thou ánsweredst thém;
A Gód forgíving | Thou wást to thém;
While púnishing their déeds.
9 *Exált ye Jáhve our Gód*
And bów at the Moúnt of His hóliness
For HÓLY IS JÁHVE our Gód.

We must now consider instances in which the
strophe is not marked either by alphabetical arrangement or by a refrain but determined only by a careful
study of the contents, e.g. Ps. xiii. Here the metre
is in four beats except for the third line where a
marginal gloss seems to have crept into the text
making the line too long.

It may be well first to offer a translation and
then to consider how far we are justified in dividing
the Psalm into strophes.

(Ps. xiii. Metre 4 + 4.)

Sorrow {
a How lóng wilt Thou útterly forgét me, Jáhve?
b How lóng wilt Thou híde Thy coúntenance fróm
me?
c How lóng must I láy distréss to mínd?
[*Gloss. grief in my heart all day.*]
d How lóng shall mine énemy exált himself agáinst
me?
}

8—2

Prayer $\begin{cases} a_1 \\ b_1 \\ c_1 \\ d_1 \end{cases}$

a_1 Regárd Thou and ánswer me, Jáhve my Gód.

b_1 Líghten mine éyes lest I sléep in déath.

c_1 Lét not mine énemy sáy, I have mástered him.

d_1 [Lét not] my fóes exúlt at my fáll.

Joy $\begin{cases} a_2 \\ b_2 \\ c_2 \\ d_2 \end{cases}$

a_2 As for mé in Thy kíndness I trúst—

b_2 My heárt exúlts in Thý salvátion—

c_2 I síng unto Jáhve for His boúnty towárds me—

d_2 (*Missing, but see Septuagint.*)

It is evident that the Psalm falls naturally into three parts. The first four lines are all *sorrow*, the second four lines are all *prayer*, and the last three lines are all *joy*. But, if our theory be right, we should have expected four lines also in the last strophe. And here the Septuagint comes to our aid and supplies exactly the line that we require to conclude the third strophe and to complete the parallelism. Thus:

"*I give práise to the Náme of Jáhve most Hígh.*"

Undoubtedly this represents the original text. Thus we have three strophes of four lines each, conveying by their arrangement the spiritual lesson that *sorrow* is turned into *joy* through *prayer*.

But further. I think we may trace a relation between the lines which I have marked *abcd*, $a_1 b_1 c_1 d_1$, $a_2 b_2 c_2 d_2$. Thus: The *Sorrow* in *a* and *b* is on account of the *hiding of God's countenance*, i.e. it is *sorrow from God*. The *sorrow* in *c* and *d* is on account of the *oppression of enemies*, i.e. it is *sorrow from man*.

So the *Prayer* in a_1 and b_1 is for the *restoration of God's countenance*; while, in c_1 and d_1 it is *deliverance from enemies*. So, too, the *Joy* in a_2 and b_2 is a thanksgiving for the *restoration of God's favour*, while in c_2 and d_2 it refers to the *benefit received through deliverance from foes*.

As to the word in line 3 which (following the Syriac) I translate "*distress*," the Hebrew has a similar word which signifies "*counsel*." I suggest that this difficult line gave rise to an early gloss "*grief in my heart* &c.," and that this gloss became incorporated in the text.

The beautiful Shepherd-Psalm (xxiii.) which is, perhaps, more familiar than any other Psalm in the Psalter, will reveal new beauties to us if we carefully study its structure. The main division of the Psalm at the close of verse 3 is obvious even to a careless reader. But the relation between the two strophes thus obtained is not generally understood and our present division into verses tends to obscure it. The metre of the Hebrew is elegiac, or *Ḳinah* measure, with an additional *stichos* in *v.* 4ᵃ which may, or may not, be due to a gloss.

In strophe I (*vv.* 1—3) we see the Good Shepherd caring for the sheep in three ways, (*a*) *by His Presence*, (*b*) *by feeding it*, (*c*) *by guiding it*. Thus it will be seen that the three lines of strophe I may be summed up under the heads *Presence, Refreshment, Guidance*.

In strophe II (*vv.* 4—6) each line of strophe I is
expanded into two lines with the same thoughts of
Presence, Refreshment and *Guidance.* For the
spiritual lessons which follow from this arrangement
I may perhaps be allowed to refer to *Psalms in Three
Collections,* Part I, pp. 104 ff.

(Ps. xxiii.   Metre 3 + 2.)

STROPHE I.

Presence	1	Jáhve's my Shépherd—I wánt not. | 'Mid vér-dure He ténds me;
Refreshment	2ᵇ	By réstful stréams He léads me; | He restóreth my sóul;
Guidance	3	He guídeth in páths that are ríght; | for His ówn Name's sáke.

STROPHE II.

Presence	⎧4	Though I gó through the Válley of Glóom | no évil I féar; | for Thoú art besíde me;
	⎩	Thy ród and Thy stáying-stáff; | théy are my cómfort.
Refreshment	⎧5	Thou spréadest a táble for mé, | in the síght of my fóes;
	⎩	Thou enríchest my héad with oíl, | my cúp overflóws!
Guidance	⎧6	Naught but góodness and mércy pursúe me | all the dáys of my lífe;
	⎩	I am hómed in the Hoúse of Jáhve, | for éver and éver!

One further illustration of the way in which the
meaning of a passage is brought out by the study of

its strophical arrangement may be given from the
beautiful song in Is. xi. 1—8. I translate from the
critical text omitting v. 3ᵃ as an obvious gloss (with
Bickell, Cheyne, Duhm, &c.).

      1 There cómeth a Shóot from Jésse-stem,
          And a Bránch buds fórth from his róots:
      2 And there résteth on hím Jahve's Spírit:—

(a)   The Spírit of Wísdom and Understánding,
(b)   The Spírit of Coúnsel and Stréngth,
(c)   The Spírit of Knówledge and Píety;

(a₁) { 3 That he júdge not by síght of his éyes;
      {   Nor convíct by the sénse of his éars,

(b₁) { 4 And he júdges the féeble with ríght;
      {   And jústly cónvicts for the póor.

(c₁) {   And he smíteth the týrant with ród of moúth;
      {   And sláyeth the wícked with bréath of his líps.

(a₂) { 5 And ríght is the gírdle of his loíns;
      {   And fáithfulness the gírdle of his réins.

(b₂) { 6 And the wólf shall lódge with the lámb;
      {   And the léopard lie dówn with the kíd.

(c₂) {   And the cálf and the líon shall pásture (together);
      {   And a líttle chíld may léad them.

(a₃) { 7 And theców and the beár shall gráze;
      {   Their yoúng-ones lie dówn togéther.

(b₃) { 8 And the líon like the óx eats háy;
      {   And the báby spórts by the ásp-hole.

(c₃) {   And óver the dén of the básilisk
      {   The wéaned-child láys his hánd.

If this passage be carefully studied it will be seen
that it is ruled by the numbers *three* and *six*. Each

of the three lines which I have marked (a), (b), (c)
contains two gifts of the Spirit. These three lines
are developed in three strophes of six lines each
which run in pairs corresponding more or less closely
with the gifts of the Spirit in the lines (a), (b), (c). I
have indicated these relations by the letters a_1, b_1, c_1;
a_2, b_2, c_2; a_3, b_3, c_3.

The arrangement in verses is quite wrong and
tends to obscure the meaning. Thus the omission of
the gloss 3[a], which we omitted on purely critical
grounds, is also defended by the structure of the
poem.

CHAPTER VII

ON DRAMATIC LYRICS

THOUGH *drama*, in the sense of the acted play, is alien to the spirit of Hebrew poetry, yet it is not so with the *dramatic lyric* which vividly pictures a scene and introduces change of thought and speaker, indicated, at times, by a change of metre. We may illustrate this from the *Song of Songs*, generally called the *Song of Solomon*. Probably no two commentators would agree as to the interpretation of the poem in every detail, but all would admit that it consists of a series of dramatic lyrics which may be divided into Acts and that it thus approximates more nearly to the *drama* than any other poem in the literature of the Bible.

The outline is briefly as follows. A beautiful Shulammite (cf. *Shunammite*, 1 K. i. 3) maiden is taken into the royal harem, where, in spite of all temptation, she remains true to the shepherd-lover of her northern home, and is at last permitted to return to him as his spotless bride, thus to vindicate the worth of love (viii. 6 ff.).

In the translations which I give as specimens of this poem I have availed myself of Rothstein's Hebrew text in his *Grundzüge des hebräischen Rhythmus*, though I have not always accepted his emendations.

In chap. i. 9—14 we have to distinguish the speakers by the context and the structure of the strophe. Thus:

Solomon is flattering the maiden.

9 To a stéed in a Pháraoh's cháriot, | I compáre thee my lóve.
10 Fáir were thy chéeks with the péarl-rings, | thy néck with the jéwels:
11 We wíll máke for thee stríngs of góld | with poínts of sílver.

Throughout this strophe the king keeps up his somewhat coarse simile of the steed with its trappings. All he has to give is gold and silver.

In the next strophe the maiden replies with modesty. She wonders that she should have found favour with the king, but assures him that she has given her love elsewhere. If *her* perfume has reached to the king, she herself knows one who, to her, is sweeter than all myrrh. Thus:

12 Can it bé to the kíng on his dívan | my pérfume hath réached?
13 My trúe-love's the búndle of mýrrh | that líes in my bósom.
14 My trúe-love's the clúster of hénna | on the slópes of En-gédi.

(Chap. ii. 3.   Metre 3 + 2.)

The Shulammite, thinking of her absent lover.

As the ápple 'mid trées of the fórest |
    so my lóve amid yoúths.
In his shádow I jóyed as I sát |
    and his frúit was my swéet.

(Chap. ii. 8 ff.)

Another reminiscence of the maiden, picturing her lover's invitation to come forth and enjoy the spring (Metre 3+2+2).

My lóve! lo hére he cómes! | léaping on the moúntains | skípping on the hílls.

He is hére, behínd our wáll; | péering through the wíndows | gláncing through the láttice.

My lóve he spéaks and cálls me; | Ríse my dárling, | Cóme my fáir-one.

For ló, the wínter's óver; | ráin is pást; | the cóld is góne.

Flówers are séen in the éarth; | sóng-time is cóme, | the ríng-dove is héard.

The fíg-tree is ríping her bálls, | the vínes are in blóom, | gíving forth scént.

Aríse then, my dárling, my dóve, | to the cléfts of the róck, | to the cóvert of stéeps.

Shéw me thy fáce, let me héar thee; | for swéet is thy voíce, | thy coúntenance cómely.

Someone sings a vineyard song (Metre 2+2).

Cátch us the fóxes, | the fóxes so smáll,
That are spoíling the víneyards, | our víneyards in blóom.

Another brief passage in the rare metre (3 + 2 + 2) is found in chap. iv. 8—13. It seems to continue the invitation to the walk in spring (ii. 8 ff.) which we have already translated, and, like that passage, it breaks into the (2 + 2) metre of popular song.

In my translation I follow Rothstein's Hebrew text.

(Chap. iv. 8 ff.   Metre 3 + 2 + 2.)

From Lébanon cáme my bríde; | with mé from Lébanon; | from
the déns of the líons.

From the tóp of Amána look fórth, | from the tóp of Shenír, |
from the moúntains of léopards.

O bríde thou hast rávished my heárt | with a glánce of thine
éyes, | with a túrn of thy néck.

How swéet thy carésses, my bríde; | how bétter than wíne! | and
thy pérfume than spíces!

Thy líps as the hóneycomb dríp; | hóney and mílk | are únder
thy tóngue.

Thy chéeks a pómegranate órchard | with choícest of frúit; |
cámphire with spíkenard.

.   .   .   .

(He sings.)

Wáke thou Nórth-wind; | cóme thou Soúth.

Bréathe on my gárden, | that its spíces may flów.

The next specimen we shall give is a beautiful
dream in which the maiden seems to herself to have
been unkind to her true lover.

(Chap. v. 2 ff.   Metre 3 + 2.)

I slépt, but my heárt was awáke | —my belóved is knócking!

"Ópen, my síster, my lóve, | my dóve, my perféction:

For my héad is fílled with déw, | my lócks with the dríp."

"As for mé I have pút off my dréss; | hów can I clóthe me?

As for mé I have wáshen my féet; | hów can I soíl them?"

He pút forth his hánd from the dóor; | my compássions were
móved.

I róse, even Í, to ópen; | and my hánds dripped with mýrrh.

Then Í, for my lóve, did ópen; | but my lóve he was góne!

My soúl went fórth at his pássing; | I cálled, but no ánswer!

The maiden finally rejects her royal admirer and declares her loyalty to her true lover (vii. 11):

My lóve he is míne, and I hís; | his desíre is to mé.

After which the metre changes back to the metre of chap. ii. 8 ff. (i.e. $3 + 2 + 2$) and the maiden accepts that invitation of her shepherd-lover almost in the words in which it had been proposed:

Cóme thou, my lóve, let us fórth; | let us dwéll in the hénna; | let us vísit the víneyards;
Let us sée if the víne hath búdded; | if its blóssom be ópen; | if the pómegranates blóom.

These three examples which we have given are, I believe, the only instances of this metre occurring in the Song.

We must conclude with the scene, chap. viii. 5—7, which is so admirably described in Dr Harper's *Commentary on the Song of Solomon* that I must borrow his words:

"The scene depicted in these verses is the return of the Shulammite with her lover to the village. As they draw near she leans upon him in weariness, and they are observed by some of the villagers, who ask the question in *v.* 5ª. The lovers meantime come slowly on, and as they come he points out an apple tree under which he had once found her sleeping and awaked her, and then as they come in sight of it, he points to her birthplace, her mother's home. In *vv.* 6 and 7 the Shulammite utters that great panegyric of love which is the climax and glory of the book. Because of this power of love which she feels in her heart she beseeches her lover to bind her closely to himself."

(viii. 5 ff.)

Scene near the village home.   Villagers speak.

5   Who is thís that comes úp from the wílderness, | that léans on her lóver ?

The bridegroom speaks to the bride.

'Twas únder (yon) ápple I wáked thee—
'Twas thére thy móther báre thee—
'Twas thére she báre thee with trávail.

The bride speaks, clinging closer to her lover.

6   Set mé as a séal on thine heárt;
(Set mé) as a séal on thine árm;
For lóve is stróng as déath;
Jéalousy is crúel as the gráve ;
It flámes with a Gód-like fláme.

*The villagers draw the moral of the bride's constancy—
speaking in prose.*

7   Many waters cannot quench love, neither can rivers drown it.   If a man would give the whole substance of his house for love he would be utterly despised.

On *v.* 6 Dr Harper well quotes Browning's *Any Wife to any Husband* :

"It would not be because my eye grew dim
   Thou couldst not find the love there, thanks to Him
      Who never is dishonoured in the spark
   He gave us from His fire of fires, and bade
   Remember whence it sprang, nor be afraid
      While that burns on, though all the rest grow dark."

Another example of the dramatic lyric may be given from the Songs of Isaiah.

Isaiah is specially fond of *paronomasia* and *assonance* (e.g. v. 7, x. 30, &c.) which he uses with great effect. He is not afraid also to use the language of mythology. Thus we cannot understand his song on *Ariél* without being reminded that the sound of the word would, to the Hebrew ear, suggest two thoughts, (*a*) "*the Lion of God,*" (*b*) "*altar-hearth*" for sacrifice, and also that the word *Dôd* might be taken either as the name *David,* or in its original significance as the divine name, as on the Moabite Stone. See Bennett's note on the Moabite Stone in *Hast. Dict.*, p. 407, where he calls attention to the fact that in the three or four places in which *Ariél* occurs "it is connected with the City of David in Is. xxix. 1 and with DWDH here." The sense of *Ariél* as an "altar-hearth" will be found in Ezek. xliii. 15 f.

The Song on Ariêl (Is. xxix. 1 ff.) opens, I believe, with the boastful words of the enemy (? Sennacherib) as follows:

1 Alás! Ariél, Ariél; | Cíty where Dôd encámps!
   Ádd (but) yéar unto yéar; | let the séasons go roúnd:

2   Thén do I stráiten Ariél,   [i.e. *God's Lion*]
    And móaning and gróaning shall bé:
    And to mé she becómes Ariél.   [i.e. *an altar-hearth*]
3   And I cámp like Dód agáinst thee,
    And lay siége with a moúnd agáinst thee,
    And ráise up agáinst thee tówers.
4   Till thou spéak, being abásed, from the groúnd,
    Thy spéech coming thín from the dúst;
    And thy voíce be as ghóst from the groúnd,
    Thy whíspering wórds from the dúst.

Here the scene changes and God speaks and assures His City of His protection. The metre here also changes. Thus:

5   Then the hóst of thy fóes | becómeth small-dúst,
    And as drífting cháff | the hóst of thy týrants:
    And thís shall be súdden and ínstant.

Here again the scene changes. No longer do we hear the words of God but the Prophet himself describes the deliverance that he sees in the vision of prophecy. Thus:

6   By Jáhve of Hósts she is vísited,
    With thúnder, and éarthquake, and míghty-voíce;
    With whírlwind, témpest, and devoúring fláme.

It is evident from the words which follow that the "visitation" of God is for the redemption of His City and for the destruction of the "multitude of the nations that fight against Ariêl" (*v.* 7).

The names Dôd, Dôdu, David are the same, and signify *Love* or the *Beloved*. The Jebusite stronghold may very possibly have been regarded as "*the City of Dôdu*" before it was taken by David and called after his own name (2 S. v. 7).

There is another Song of Isaiah's in which he appears to me to use *Dôdu* as a name of God. It is the *Song of the Vineyard* (v. 1 ff.).

Lét me now síng for Dódu | Dódu's sóng of his víneyard.
Dôdu hád a víneyard | on a híll very fértile.
And he fénced it, and cléared it and plánted it choícely.
And he buílt thereín a tówer,
And álso héwed him a wíne-vat.
So he lóoked it should yiéld him grápes—
      And it yiélded but wíld-grapes!

Thus we have the "*City* of David" and the *Vineyard* (or *Vine*) of David. The *Vine* was the emblem of Judah (Ezek. xv. ; Gen. xlix. 11; Ps. lxxx. 8—14) and I suggest that the difficult passage in *The Teaching of the Twelve Apostles*, Ch. ix., respecting the "*Vine of David*" had its origin in Isaiah's *Song of the Vine* or *Song of the Vineyard*, for the word may be translated either way.

The passage in the "Teaching" runs thus :

"Now, concerning the Eucharist, thus shall ye give thanks. First with regard to the Cup :—We give thanks to Thee, our Father, for the holy Vine (of) David Thy Servant which Thou madest known unto us through Jesus Thy Servant." The Suffering Servant is the "very vine" of God (Jn. xv. 1—5).

K.   9

The second Psalm may be given as a good illustration of Dramatic Lyrics, though we might have been equally justified in regarding it as an example of the strophe. The change of speaker is vividly distinguished by the context. Thus, in *v.* 3 we have the rebel words of the earth-powers; in *v.* 6 the words of God with respect to His Anointed ; while, in *vv.* 7—9, the Anointed himself speaks of his God-given authority. Thus there is a relation between strophes II and III, while strophe IV exactly corresponds with strophe I. I have left the difficult line *v.* 12ᵃ untranslated because this is not the place for a critical investigation of the text. The corresponding reference to the "Christ" in *v.* 2, and to the "Son" in *v.* 7, would lead us to expect some such line as, "Obey the Son lest he be angry and ye perish." It is only fair to say that the text as it stands is uncertain on critical grounds and does not quite suit the metre.

(Psalm ii.)

STROPHE I. *The Voice of the Psalmist.*

1 Whý do the héathen ráge | and the péoples váinly desígn?
2 The kíngs of the éarth stand úp | and prínces are bánded
    togéther
        'Gainst Jáhve and 'gáinst His Chríst!
3 "Let us breák asúnder their bónds | and cást from óff us their
    fétters."

STROPHE II. *The scene in heaven.*

4 The thróned-One in héaven láughs ; | the Lórd but derídes them !

5 He spéaketh to thém in His ánger | and troúbleth thém in His wráth.

6 " 'Twas Í that anoínted My Kíng | on Zíon My hóly Moúnt."

STROPHE III. *The Voice of the Anointed.*

7 Let me téll of Jáhve's decrée—
He sáid to me, Thoú art My Són, | it is Í, this dáy, have begótten thee.

8 Ásk of Mé that I gíve thee | nátions thine héritage, | the énds of the éarth thy posséssion.

9 Thou shalt breák them with scéptre of íron, | as a pótter's véssel shalt shátter them.

STROPHE IV. *The Voice of the Psalmist.*

10 And nów, ye kíngs, be wíse; | be wárned ye júdges of éarth.

11 Sérve ye Jáhve with féar; | and...unto Hím with trémbling.

12 .   .   .   .
For his ánger may éasily búrn. | Happy théy that take réfuge in Hím.

CHAPTER VIII

THE POETRY OF THE SEASONS

To every poet the spring of the year is a prophecy of new creation. Shelley felt this when he wrote:

"The airs and streams renew their joyous tone;
  The ants, the bees, the swallows, reappear;
  Fresh leaves and flowers deck the dead season's bier.
  The loving birds now pair in every brake,
  And build their mossy homes in field and brere;
  And the green lizard and the golden snake,
  Like unimprison'd flames, out of their trance awake,
  Through wood and stream, and field and hill and ocean,
  A quickening life from the earth's heart has burst,
  As it has ever done, with change and motion,
  From the great morning of the world! when first
  God dawn'd on chaos: ...."

No wonder then, if to the Hebrew poet, who was, before all things, a prophet, the cycle of the seasons shall speak of God's eternal purpose for His worlds.

It would not be difficult to shew that the "Days" of Creation (Gen. i.) are based upon the months of the year, commencing from the spring, which, as Shelley reminds us, is the type of "the great morning of the world." In a little book like this I cannot do more than suggest a few thoughts on this wide and important subject. For this purpose I commence with Ps. civ. and must repeat, in part, what I have written in my Introduction to that Psalm (*Psalms in Three Collections*, p. 430).

The Psalm is based upon the "Six Days" of Creation as given in the Priest-code (Gen. i.). There is, however, this important difference that, whereas Gen. i. purposes to relate in prose the order of life's first beginnings, our Psalmist, with a poet's instinct, recognises Creation as an eternal work which is still going on and which all points to a "far off Divine Event," viz. the completion of God's joy in His works. This being so he sees no inconsistency in regarding animals, birds and men as being already in existence on the Third Day. We might analyse the Psalm as follows:

vv. 1, 2. The First Day, like the first month in spring, is filled with the promise of the birth of light.

vv. 3, 4. The Second Day reminds us how God builds His firmament, making, as Shelley says,

"...the winds and sunbeams, with their convex gleams
    Build up the blue dome of air,"

thus causing the very elements of destruction to contribute to the conservation of the earth.

vv. 5—18. The Third Day, like the third month, is "the gift of seed." It reminds us how (*a*) God has taken the waters, which were once the winding-sheet of a dead earth, and made them countless rills of blessing to birds and beasts and men. It also reminds us (*b*) how God made the dry land thus to become the bountiful seed-plot of corn and wine and oil.

vv. 19—23. The Fourth Day, like the fourth month (the month of the summer stolstice) tells God's good purpose in darkness as well as in light, while it points to the final triumph of light (*v.* 22 f.).

vv. 24—30. The Fifth Day, like the fifth month (which even in the nature-religion of Babylonia was dedicated to Istar as the *bona dea* of fertility), tells of the infinite variety of God's "creatures" and of His care for all their needs.

vv. 31—35. The Sixth Day, like the autumn month, sums up the growing purpose of the whole Creation, viz. that this bountiful God may rejoice at last in a world from which all evil has been expelled.

The metre of the Psalm is $3 + 3$ with occasional triplets.

(Ps. civ.)

The First "Day" of Creation (Gen. i. 3—5). *Voices of Spring.*

1 Thou art greát, O my Gód, excéedingly : | Thou hast déck'd Thee with spléndour and májesty.

2 Pútting on líght as a gárment; | spréading out the héavens as a cúrtain.

The Second "Day" of Creation (Gen. i. 6—8). *God's Building seen in the Firmament* (cf. Ps. xix. 2).

3 ⎰He flóoreth His upper-chámbers in the wáters;
  ⎱He máketh thick cloúds His cháriot;
  ⎰He móveth on wíngs of the wínd.

4 Máking the wínds His ángels | the fláming fíre His mínisters.

The Third "Day" of Creation (Gen. i. 9 f.). *Dry land and seed.*

5 He foúnded the éarth on her báses; | that she shoúld not be móved for éver.

6 With the Déep, as a gárment, Thou hast cóvered her; | so the wáters stood óver the moúntains.

7 At Thý rebúke they flée ;—
  At the voíce of Thy thúnder they hásten :—

8ᵇ To the pláce Thou hadst foúnded for thém :

9 Nor transgréss the límit assígned them, | nor retúrn to cóver the éarth.

10 He séndeth the spríngs down the chánnels ; | amóng the moúntains they rún.

11 They give drínk to all béasts of the fiéld ; | wild-ásses may quénch their thírst.

13 He gives moúntains to drínk from His chámbers ; | Earth is fílled from the frúit of Thy wórks.

14 Making gráss to spríng for the cáttle | and hérbage for tíllage of mán.

15 To bríng forth fóod from the éarth | and wíne that may gládden man's heárt.

  Chéering the fáce with oíl | and fóod that should stréngthen man's heárt.

16 The trées of Gód have their fíll ; | the cédars of Lébanon that He plánted.

12 On thém dwell fówls of héaven: | 'mid their bránches they
    útter their sóng.
17 'Tis thére the líttle-birds nést; | the stórk (too) whose hóme
    is the fírs.
18 The lófty hílls for the góats; | the crágs are a réfuge for the
    cónies.

The Fourth "Day" of Creation (Gen. i. 14—19). *The lesser
and greater lights. The cycle of the festivals.*

19 He máketh the móon for the séasons; | and the sún knows
    the pláce of his sétting.
20 Thou mákest dárkness—it is níght— | all béasts of the
    fórest creep fórth.
21 The líons róaring for préy | and séeking their méat from Gód.
22 The sún but ríses—they are góne, | and láy them dówn in
    their déns.
23 Mán goeth fórth to his wórk, | to his lábour untíl the
    évening.

The Fifth "Day" of Creation (Gen. i. 20—23). *The voices
of summer. The teeming life of earth and sea.*

24 O Jáhve, how greát are Thy wórks!
    The whóle Thou hast wróught in wísdom!
    The éarth is fílled with Thy wéalth!
25 This séa, so greát and wide-spréading,
    Whereín are things créeping innúmerable;
    Creátures both smáll and greát.
26 Thére the shíps [? *the nautili*] go alóng | and Levíathan
    fórmed for Thy pláything.
27 They áll look expéctant to Thée | to gíve them their fóod in
    its séason.
28 Thou gívest to thém—they gáther it: | Thou ópenest Thy
    hánd—they are sáted.

29 Thou hídest Thy Fáce—they are troúbled :
    Thou withdráwest their bréath—they expíre,
    And retúrn agáin to their dúst.
30 Thou séndest Thy bréath—they are máde— | Thou renéwest
        the fáce of the groúnd.

The poet now draws his conclusion as a prophet
from the cycle of God's work which he has traced in
creation. He would not have said with the Writer
of Ecclesiastes that "what has been shall be and that
there is nothing new under the sun." On the contrary
he sees that God is making all things new. He sees
that God's purpose is good and that life not death is
the end (*v.* 30).

> That nothing walks with aimless feet;
> That not one life shall be destroyed,
> Or cast as rubbish to the void,
> When God hath made the pile complete.

So the conclusion to which our Psalmist arrives is
based upon that first Sixth Day (Gen. i. 24—31), when
God looked upon all things that He had made and
declared them to be " very good."

As God then rejoiced in His works, so God will
rejoice in the End which must mean the extinction of
all evil.

*The Sixth " Day" of Creation and its meaning for the future—
    Autumn voices. Every common bush a-flame with God.*

31 Be the Glóry of Jáhve for éver ! | Let Jáhve rejoíce in His
        wórks !

32 Who but lóoketh on éarth and it trémbleth; | He but toúcheth
    the hílls and they smóke.
33 I will síng while I líve unto Jáhve; | While being lásts I will
    hýmn to my Gód.
34 My músing on Hím shall be swéet: | As for mé I rejoíce in
    Jáhve.
35 May sínners be énded from éarth, | and the wícked exíst no
    móre !
    My sóul do thoú bless Jáhve.

Even in the early days of the Jehovist the promise
that "seed-time and harvest, cold and heat, summer
and winter, day and night, should not cease," was
given as the pledge of God's acceptance (Gen. viii. 22).

The order of the seasons was, to the prophet
Jeremiah, a token of God's everlasting covenant with
Israel.   Thus, Jer. xxxiii. 20 f.: "Thus saith Jahve,
If ye can break My covenant, the day, and My cove-
nant, the night, so that day and night should not be
in their season; then may also My covenant with
David, My servant, be broken...."

And again, *v.* 25 f.: "If I did not appoint My
covenant the day and the night as laws of heaven
and earth; then, too, I might cast off the seed of
Jacob and David My servant." The reader will
notice that the Covenant of Creation becomes the
pledge of the Covenant with David.

Jeremiah's famous chapter (xxxi.) on the New
Covenant closes with the same thought, *vv.* 35—37
(Heb. 34—36): "Thus saith Jahve that giveth the

sun for light by day, the laws of the moon and stars for light by night...If these laws can depart from before Me, saith Jahve, then might the seed of Israel cease from being a nation before Me for ever...." The poet of the next generation, known to us as the Second Isaiah, connects this Covenant of Creation with the Covenant of Noah, Is. liv. 9, "For this is unto Me the waters of Noah, even as I have sworn that the waters of Noah should not again pass over the earth so have I sworn not to be angry with thee (Israel) and not to rebuke thee."

About a hundred years later the author of the Priest Code interprets for us the "waters of Noah" by the rainbow sign of God's Covenant with the earth (Gen. ix. 8—17).

In the Asaph Psalm lxxiv. the Psalmist appeals to God by the Covenant of Creation, to fulfil His promise which seems to be delayed. The whole passage should be studied; we can but quote *vv.* 13—17 which refer to the Covenant of Creation. The emphatic use of the pronoun *Thou* should be noticed and also the reference to the first four "Days of Creation." Thus:

*Day I. Light, or the smiting of the dragon of darkness;
as in the Babylonian story.*

Thoú with Thy pówer | didst breák the séa,
Didst shíver the héads | of the drágons on the wáters.

*Day II.   The Firmament.   The chaos of waters divided;
as in the Babylonian story.*

THOÚ didst rénd | the héads of Levíathan,
Didst gíve him as fóod | to the désert fólk.

Day III.   Waters in one place; dry land appears.

THOÚ didst cléave | foúntain and bróok;
THOÚ didst drý | perénnial rívers.

Day IV.   The greater and lesser lights.

Thíne is the dáy, | Thíne, too, the níght;
THOÚ didst estáblish | the líghts and the sún.

The Covenant of Creation with reference to Gen. viii. 22.

THOÚ didst appoínt | all boúndaries of éarth ;
Súmmer and wínter, | THOÚ it was didst fórm them.

It will be seen that in this Psalm the metre is
2 + 2 and, if we compare the closely parallel Psalm
lxxxix., the study of metre opens up a most interesting
question.   For, in Ps. lxxxix. the metre, for the most
part, is the common one of 3 + 3, but it contains
passages of 2 + 2 metre;   and it appears to me that
these latter passages all refer to the Covenant of
Creation, while the passages in 3 + 3 metre refer to
the Covenant of David.

I shall endeavour to represent the change of metre
in my translation and must leave the reader to judge
whether two independent Psalms have been combined
or whether the writer wished to place side by side
the Covenant of David and the Covenant of Creation
and varied his metre to suit his subject.

(Ps. lxxxix.)

Metre 2+2. *Covenant of Creation.*

(*a*) 2 I síng the etérnal | mércies of Jáhve.
(*b*)   I make knówn with my moúth | Thy faíthfulness for áges.
(*a₁*) 3 I saíd, as etérnal, | mércy shall be buílt.
(*b₁*)   As the héavens Thou estáblishest | (so) Thy faíthfulness therein.

Metre 3+3. *The David Covenant.*

4 A cóvenant I máde with My chósen ;
   I swáre unto Dávid My sérvant,
5 Thy séed I estáblish for éver ;
   And buíld up thy thróne for all áges.

It will be seen that though the metre is different the language and thought is identical with that in *vv.* 2, 3. It would seem that the writer wished, like Jeremiah, to place the "sure mercies of David" side by side with the sure mercies of Creation. The metre now changes back to that of *vv.* 2, 3.

Metre 2+2. *Covenant of Creation.*

6 For the héavens shall práise | Thy wónder-work, Jáhve ;
   Thy faíthfulness too | in cóncourse of Hóly-ones.
7 For whó, in high-héaven, | compáreth with Jáhve ?
   Whó matcheth Jáhve | 'mid sóns of the góds ?
8 A Gód revéred | in assémbly of Hóly-ones ;
   Greát and to be féared | by áll that are aroúnd Him.
   .   .   .   .
10 Thoú dost lórd it | o'er the príde of the séa ;
   When his wáves are uplífted, | Thoú layest to rést.
11 'Twas Thoú that didst crúsh | proud-Ráhab as sláin,
   With the árm of Thy míght | didst scátter Thine énemies.

12 Thíne are the héavens; | Thíne too the éarth.
    The wórld and its fúlness; | THOÚ (it was) didst foúnd them.
13 The nórth and the soúth; | THOÚ (it was) créated them.
    Tábor and Hérmon | ríng with Thy náme.
14 Thíne is the árm; | Thíne is the pówer.
    Stróng is Thy hánd; | Hígh is Thy ríght-hand.
15 Ríghteousness and júdgement | the foundátion of Thy thróne,
    Mércy and trúth | that gó before Thy fáce.

The reader will note how exactly *vv.* 10 ff. correspond with the verses we have already translated
from Ps. lxxiv.: the same metre, the same mythology,
the same reference to the "Days" of Creation, the
same remarkable use of the emphatic "THOU."

We now pass to verse 20 which is pure prose as
follows:

"Thou spakest of old in a vision with Thy saints
[or, possibly, '*with respect to Thy Saint*'] and didst
say;—"

These words form an introduction to the Promise
which continues as follows:

Metre 3+3. *David Covenant.*

20 I have sét a crówn(?) on a héro;
    Have exálted one chósen of the péople.
21 I foúnd Me Dávid My sérvant;
    With Thy hóly oíl I anoínted him.
22 That My hánd, should bé his stáy;
    And mine árm should gíve him stréngth.
23 That the énemy shoúld not exáct;
    Nor the wícked one caúse him afflíction.

24 I will béat down his fóes before hím,
       Will smíte them that háte him.
25 While with hím is My trúth and My mércy,
       In My náme shall his hórn be exálted.
26 And I sét his hánd on the séa,
       His right-hánd on the rívers.
27 He námes Me, Thoú art my Fáther,
       My Gód and my Róck-Salvátion.
28 While Í too appoínt him My fírstborn,
       A Most Hígh to the kíngs of the éarth.
29 My mércy I kéep his for éver,
       And for hím is My cóvenant stáblished.
30 And I máke his séed etérnal,
       His thróne as the dáys of héaven.
31 Should his sóns forsáke My láw,
       So as nót to wálk in My júdgements,
32 Shoúld they profáne My státutes
       So as nót to obsérve My commándments,
33 Then I vísit their transgréssion with a ród,
       And with scoúrges their sín.
34 Yet from hím I remóve not My mércy;
       Nor wíll I prove fálse to My fáithfulness.
35 My Cóvenant wíll I not breák;
       Nor chánge what My líps have annoúnced.
36 Once for áll have I swórn by My hóliness
       That I néver prove fálse to Dávid.
37 His séed shall bé for éver,
       And his thróne as the sún befóre Me.
38 It shall stáy as the móon for éver,
       And the wítness that is fáithful in the ský.

The Psalm continues *in the same metre* to plead
with God (as Ps. lxxiv.) the non-performance of His

promises, until we come to the last two verses (51, 52) where it would seem to break once more into the (2 + 2) metre which we have already found in *vv.* 2, 3, 6—15. Thus:

51   Remémber O Lórd | the repróach of Thy sérvant;
     How I beár in my bósom | the sháme of the Péoples:
52   Wherewíth they repróach— | Thine énemies, Jáhve!—
     Wherewíth they repróach | the fóotsteps of Thy Chríst.

The text, however, in these two verses is by no means certain.

I propose, in the present chapter, to examine one aspect of the spring, which is summed up under the Hebrew word *Tzemach*, a word signifying that "*outspring*" from the earth, which results from the spring of the year. It is most unfortunate that, in the E.V., this word should have been translated "*Branch*," thus hiding from the English reader a very beautiful and suggestive thought.

In the passages which follow I shall indicate the root *Tzemach*, whether as a *verb* or as a *substantive*, by giving the translation in italics.

(Is. iv. 2.)

In that day there shall be
The *outspring* of Jahve as a beauty and pride,
And the fruit of the land as a glory and boast
For the remnant of Israel.

Here the "*outspring of Jahve*" answers to the "*fruit of the Land*" in the parallel line. It is called the "*outspring of Jahve*" because He makes it *to spring forth* as it is said of Paradise, Gen. ii. 9, "And out of the ground Jahve Elohim *made to spring* every tree that was pleasant to the sight and good for food."

Such was the *intention* of God in Creation. This intention was hindered by the Fall in which Earth is represented as sympathising. "Thorns also and thistles shall it (i.e. the Earth) *make to spring for* thee" (Gen. iii. 18). But, though hindered, the purpose of God still remains and is manifested in the parable of every spring. It is He who "*maketh* the grass *to spring* for the cattle" (Ps. civ. 14); "*causing* the mountains *to spring* with grass" (Ps. cxlvii. 8).

But, in another sense, the earth may be said to "bring forth fruit of itself"; consequently *Tzemach* may be applied to the earth ; and, as such, it is frequently used collectively, e.g. Ezek. xvi. 7 "*the outspring* (E.V. *the bud*) of the field*"; Hos. viii. 7 "*the outspring* (E.V. *bud*) shall yield no meal."

These two closely related thoughts must be borne in mind, forming, as they do, a parable of the Christ. The "*outspring*" is God's, inasmuch as He, the "Sun of Righteousness," makes it to grow. But the "*outspring*" is the earth's since the earth "bringeth forth fruit of itself."

The Second Isaiah expresses a similar thought only that, in his case, the picture is not that of a *Sun* of righteousness but rather of a *rain* of righteousness from heaven which the thirsty earth should drink in and thereby become fruitful (cf. Hos. x. 12). Thus:

(Is. xlv. 8.)

> Ye héavens shower dówn from abóve,
> Ye skíes pour dówn with Ríghteousness,
> Let them frúit with Salvátion—earth ópen,
> Let Ríghteousness *spring forth* at ónce,
> I, Jáhve, Í have creáted it.

Again,

(Is. lxi. 11.)

> For as éarth brings fórth her *oútspring*,
> And as gárden makes séeds to *spring oút*,
> So Jáhve *makes* Ríghteousness *spring*,
> Even práise before áll the nátions.

Jeremiah associates this thought of the "outspring" with a personal Deliverer of the family of David.

(Jer. xxiii. 5 f.)

> Behóld the dáys are cóming, saith Jáhve,
> That I ráise up for Dávid a ríghteous *oútspring*,
> And a Kíng shall réign and prósper,
> And shall éxecute júdgement and ríghteousness on éarth.
> In hís days shall Júdah be sáved,
> And Ísrael dwéll in secúrity:
> And thís is his náme they shall cáll (him)
> > Jáhve our Ríghteousness.

(Jer. xxxiii. 15.)

I ráise up for Dávid an *oútspring* of ríghteousness
And he shall éxecute júdgement and ríghteousness on éarth.
In thóse days shall Júdah be sáved,
And Jerúsalem dwéll in secúrity:
And thís is whát they shall cáll (it)
Jáhve our Ríghteousness.

If we may trust the text in these closely
related passages, we see that while one speaks of a
"*righteous outspring*," who is himself to be called
"*Jahve our righteousness*," the other speaks of an
"*out-spring of righteousness*" in the earth, which is
to bear the Name of Him who produces it, and is to be
called "Jahve our righteousness." Both thoughts are
needed. In Palestine, where the winter rains were
followed by an almost tropical growth, the outburst,
the spring, was well fitted to be a parable of the
New Creation.

Thus Joel (ii. 21 ff.) says:

21 Fear nót O éarth; | be jóyful and glád,
   For Jáhve is dóing great thíngs.
22 Fear nót, ye béasts of the fiéld;
   For the pástures of the wílderness are sproúting;
   For the trées are gíving their frúit,
   Both fíg-tree and víne are yiélding their stréngth.
23 So ye chíldren of Zíon be jóyful and glád
   In Jáhve your Gód:
   For to yoú He hath gíven the ráin for ríghteousness.

There is a play upon the word *moreh*, "*rain*" in
the last line. It denotes the "*former rain*," i.e. the

heavy rain at the beginning of the winter, but it also
signifies "*a teacher*." According to the Prophet's
thought the earth and the beasts have cause to rejoice;
but the "Children of Zion" should see something
deeper in this parable of God's gift of rain which
should speak to them of the growth of righteousness.
So, too, the words which follow speak of "*the latter
rain in the first (month)*," E.V. or "*the latter rain
first of all.*" Here again a double meaning is intended: the "*latter rain*" is in the first (spring)
month, but truly it is "*first of all*" in reference to
the "*afterwards*" (*v.* 28, Heb. iii. 1) when God would
"pour out His Spirit upon all flesh." The first out-
pouring is a parable of the second. Again,

(Is. lxvii. 10 f.)

> For líke as the ráin cometh dówn
> And the snów out of héaven,
> Nor retúrneth agáin,
> Untíl it have wátered the éarth,
> And máde it to bríng forth and *spríng*;
> Gíving both séed to the sówer,
> And bréad to the éater:
> Só shall it bé with My Wórd
> That cómeth fórth from My Moúth;
> It shall nót retúrn to Me émpty,
> Untíl it have dóne what I wíll,
> And have próspered in thát which I sénd it.

In the times of the Prophet Zechariah *Tzemach*
had become personified. Thus, iii. 8: "Hear now O

Joshua the high priest, thou and thy fellows that sit before thee; for men of typical-import they are:—For behold I am going to bring My servant Tzemach —And he it is that shall build the temple of Jahve, and he it is that shall bear the dignity; and shall sit and rule upon his throne, and the counsel of peace shall be between them both."

And again, vi. 12: "Behold the man whose name is Tzemach (*the outspring*); from his own place he shall *spring up* and build the temple of Jahve."

Thus Zechariah regarded Joshua and Zerubbabel, the Temple-builders of his own day, merely as types of the true Temple-builder who was to come. This true Temple-builder he calls by the name Tzemach thereby associating him with the thoughts which we have already considered.

We must, however, briefly allude to a remarkable development of the word *Tzemach* whereby it came to denote not merely the *outspring* from the ground but the *outspring* of light, i.e. the *dayspring*. This arose, in part, from the use of ἀνατολή for *Tzemach* in the Greek versions. For ἀνατολή has both meanings; it signifies that which *springs from the ground* (see Ezek. xvi. 7, xvii. 9 f. and compare Gen. xix. 25 ; Ps. lxiv. (lxv.) 11) and also the *outspring of light*, the *dayspring* (Jer. xxiii. 5 ; xxxiii. 15, Theod. and Sym. ; Zech. iii. 8, vi. 12). In the later Hebrew and Syriac the root *Tzemach* tended

10—3

more towards the secondary meaning of the *day-spring*. Thus the "*Dayspring from on high*" (Lk. i. 78) is to be traced to the group of Tzemach prophecies.

There is a fine poetical passage in Ps. lxv. 10—14 where the course of God's bounty through the year is compared to the laden wagon of a "harvest-home," dropping its richness as its goes.

I confess I can make nothing of the metre of *vv.* 10, 11, but *vv.* 12—14 are in three beats.

10   Thou hast visited the earth and saturated her,
     Enriching her with the water-full stream of God:

    .   .   .   .

11   Watering her furrows, levelling her ridges,
     Thou mellowest her with rain-drops, Thou blessest her
        outspring.
12   Thou hast crówned the yéar of Thy góodness;
     And Thy whéel-tracks dróp with plénty.
13   They dróp on the wílderness-pástures,
     And the hílls are gírdled with jóy.
14   The méadows are clóthed with flócks;
     And the válleys are cóvered with córn;
     They shoút for jóy—yea síng.

The reader will notice the reference to *Tzemach* in *v.* 11.

Again, in the Psalm of the thrée-fold priestly Blessing (Ps. lxvii.) the pledge of the Blessing for the world is found in the fruitful season, though in this case the word *Tzemach* is not used:

            Éarth hath yiélded her íncrease;
            Gód our Gód will bléss us.

Compare also Ezek. xxxiv. 27, Zech. viii. 12. These thoughts of the earth's fertility are coupled with the advent of a Prince of Peace in Ps. lxxii., just as in the Prophets.

1 Give Thy júdgements, O Gód, to the Kíng,
     Thy ríghteousness únto the Prínce.
2 May he ríght Thy Péople with mércy,
     And Thy Póor-ones with jústice.
3 May the moúntains uplíft their péace,
     And the hílls with ríghteousness....
4 May he júdge the póor of the Péople,
     May he sáve the sóns of the néedy :—
          And crúsh the oppréssor.
5 May he léngthen out (dáys) with the sún,
     With the móon for éndless áges.
6 Coming dówn like ráin upon gráss,
     As the dróps that dríp on the éarth.
7 Ríghteousness will blóom in his dáys,
     Great péace till móons be no móre.
8 So he rúles from séa to séa,
     From the Ríver to boúnds of éarth.
9 Befóre him fóes bow dówn
     And his énemies líck the dúst.
10 The Kíngs of the Ísles and of Társhish | bríng their gífts,
     The Kíngs of Shéba and Séba | óffer their présents.
11 All Kíngs bow dówn unto hím ; | all nátions do sérvice.
12 For he frées the póor that críeth ; | the afflícted and
     hélpless.
13 He píties the póor and the néedy;
     Yea the sóuls of the néedy he sáves.
14 From víolence and wróng he redeéms them;
     And their blóod, in his síght, is précious.

15 .   .   .   .
 So the práyer for hím is contínuous; | all dáy do they bléss
  him.
16 Let the oútspread of córn be on éarth | to the tóp of the hílls.
 Let its frúitage rústle like Lébanon:
 So they blóssom [from the city[1]] as the hérbage of the éarth.
17 May his náme endúre for éver;
 May his náme incréase with the sún.

The growing light and strength of the sun through
the year is regarded as a type of the great year of
Eternity, in which the Sun of Righteousness with
increasing light will bring forth more and more fruit
from humanity.

We pass now to *vv.* 10—14 of Ps. lxxxv. where
the metre is very clearly marked in three beats. The
Psalm anticipates the return of the Divine Glory to
earth.

10 His salvátion is nígh to His féarers,
 That glóry may dwéll in our éarth.
11 Mércy and trúth are mét,
 Ríghteousness and péace have embráced.
12 Trúth from éarth *outspríngs*,
 And ríghteousness béams from Héaven.
13 So Jáhve gíves the góod,
 Our éarth, too, gíves her íncrease.
14 Ríghteousness márches befóre Him,
 And kéeps the wáy of His stéps.

 [1] I would suggest that the words "from the city," which break the
metre, were introduced, as a gloss, to bring out the thought of the
passage; the crop being not one of corn and flowers but of human
righteousness.

There is no passage in the Psalter that brings home the meaning of *Tzemach* more perfectly than this. As heaven and earth combine to produce the outcome of the seasons in the natural year, so, in God's great year, Heaven and earth will combine to produce the "man whose name is Tzemach" and the fruits of the Spirit. To this thought I would apply the words of Browning:

"And the emulous heaven yearned down,
            made effort to reach the earth,
    As the earth had done her best, in my passion
            to reach the sky."

BIBLIOGRAPHY

Briggs, C. A. *Study of Holy Scripture.*

Budde, K. *Poetry (Hebrew).* In Hastings' *Dict. of Bible.* A very useful Article.

Cobb, W. H. *A criticism of Systems of Heb. Metre* (Oxford, 1905). Contains a full bibliography up to 1904.

Cooke, G. A. *Hist. and Song of Deborah.*

Harper, A. *The Song of Solomon.*

Kautzsch, E. *Die Poesie und die poet. Bücher des Alt. Test.* (1902).

—— *Outline of hist. of Literature of O.T.* (English Translation).

—— *Edition of Proverbs with critical Heb. text.*

King, E. G. *The Psalms in three Collections* (Deighton, Bell & Co.).

König, E. *Die Poesie des alten Testaments.* Recently published. I have not yet seen this book.

Moulton, R. G. *The literary study of the Bible.*

Rothstein, J. W. *Song of Songs.* In Hastings' *Dict. of Bible.*

—— *Grundzüge des heb. Rhythmus* (Leipzig, 1909).

Zapletal, O. P. *De Poesi Hebraeorum* (1909). A hand-book of 46 pages, written in Latin for School use.

—— *Das Deboralied.*

INDEX